AYÚDANOS A LOCALIZARLOS

 JOSÉ ÁNGEL NAVARRETE GONZÁLEZ
 MARCIAL PABLO BARANDA
DANIEL GERARDO CANTÚ MORALES — Encontrado
MIGUEL ÁNGEL MENDOZA ZACARÍAS — Encontrado
 SEVERO PEDRO MINGA
JESÚS JOVANY RODRÍGUEZ TLATEMPA
EDUARDO AYAFREDO SEBASTIÁN SALGADO — Encontrado
 ABELARDO VÁZQUEZ PENITEN

 ALEXANDER MORA VENANCIO
JULIO CÉSAR RAMÍREZ NAVA
 LUIS ÁNGEL ABARCA CARRILLO
 JORGE ÁLVAREZ NAVA
ADÁN ABRAJÁN DE LA CRUZ
 MATEO CARRERA MOCTEZUMA — Encontrado
CHRISTIAN TOMÁS COLÓN GARNICA
 LUIS ÁNGEL FRANCISCO ARZOLA

 JOSÉ ÁNGEL CAMPOS CANTOR
JORGE ANÍBAL CRUZ MENDOZA
 GIOVANNI GALINDES GUERRERO
 JHOSIVANI GUERRERO DE LA CRUZ
 LUIS ÁNGEL GUTIÉRREZ ÁLVAREZ — Encontrado
CARLOS LORENZO HERNÁNDEZ MUÑOZ
 ISRAEL JACINTO LUGARDO
 JULIO CÉSAR LÓPEZ PATOLZIN

 JONATHAN MALDONADO HERNÁNDEZ — Encontrado
AMBROCIO MARTÍNEZ RODRÍGUEZ — Encontrado
 CUTBERTO ORTIZ RAMOS
EVERARDO RODRÍGUEZ BELLO
MARCO ANTONIO ANDRÉS SANTOS — Encontrado
 FELIPE ARNULFO ROSA
 BENJAMÍN ASCENCIO BAUTISTA
ISRAEL CABALLERO SÁNCHEZ

 CHRISTIAN ALFONSO RODRÍGUEZ
 MARTÍN GETSEMANY SÁNCHEZ GARCÍA
 JONÁS TRUJILLO GONZÁLEZ
 JOSÉ EDUARDO BARTOLO TLATEMPA
ABEL GARCÍA HERNÁNDEZ
 EMILIANO ALEN GASPAR DE LA CRUZ
 DORIAM GONZÁLEZ PARRAL
 JORGE LUIS GONZÁLEZ PARRAL

 LEONEL CASTRO ABARCA
 MIGUEL ÁNGEL HERNÁNDEZ MARTÍNEZ
 CARLOS IVÁN RAMÍREZ VILLAREAL
 CIRINO TEJEDA MEZA
 MAGDALENO RUBÉN LAURO VILLEGAS
 JOSÉ LUIS LUNA TORRES — Encontrado
 RODRIGO MORALES GARCÍA
 MAURICIO ORTEGA VALERIO

 JORGE ANTONIO TIZAPA LEGIDEÑO
 MARIO TORREBLANCA FLORES — Encontrado
 JAZZIEL RAMÍREZ SÁNCHEZ — Encontrado
 ANTONIO SANTANA MAESTRO
 JULIO CÉSAR VELÁZQUEZ ALONSO — Encontrado
 MARCO ANTONIO GÓMEZ MOLINA
 CÉSAR MANUEL GONZÁLEZ HERNÁNDEZ
 SAÚL BRUNO GARCÍA

 BENJAMÍN ACERGO BAUTISTA

SI HAS VISTO O SABES ALGO DE ESTAS PERSONAS, CONTÁCTANOS A TRAVÉS DE:
informaciondebusqueda@gmail.com
TEL.: (744) 485-37-98
TU LLAMADA ES ANÓNIMA Y CONFIDENCIAL

 GUERRERO GOBIERNO DEL ESTADO

SEMIOTEXT(E) INTERVENTION SERIES

© Sergio González Rodríguez, 2015. Originally published in
Spanish by Editorial Anagrama S.A.

Published by Semiotext(e)
PO BOX 629, South Pasadena, CA 91031
www.semiotexte.com

Thanks to John Ebert.

Design: Hedi El Kholti

ISBN: 978-1-58435-197-9
Distributed by The MIT Press, Cambridge, Mass.
and London, England
Printed in the United States of America

Sergio González Rodríguez

The Iguala 43

The Truth and Challenge of Mexico's Disappeared Students

Translated by Joshua Neuhouser

semiotext(e)
intervention
series □ 20

For Carlos, my guide in Guerrero,
Magdalena, Clara, Victoria and Javier

Contents

1

CONFESSION

I have wanted to avoid this, but it's impossible. I must overcome the lack of urgency that has triumphed in the language of politics and public life, and even literature and journalism. The beautiful forms that so often try to obscure reality.

I must say what nobody else wants to mention. Against silence, against hypocrisy, against lies, I must raise my voice. And I must do so because I know that there are people like me in every part of the world who share my conviction that the influence of the perverse has devoured civilization, the institutional order, the common good.

It could be argued that this is in no way true, that everything is better for humanity than it was in the past, that democracy allows each of us to climb the ladder of the perfectible, that what's expected of people is clear, that liberty has finally reached its historical climax: science, logical reasoning, the free market economy, individualization, a social contract that establishes responsibilities for both the rulers and the ruled, multilateralism in international politics.

And yet facts stubbornly emerge that contradict this deceitful discourse. And the color gray tends to impose itself on a world that once admitted the richness of the full chromatic spectrum. The unanimous gray of the ashes of those killed unjustly, of sewers and effervescent filth, of turbid bogs, of political "impartiality" and utilitarianism in the name of ideological causes.

Before I go to sleep each night, a deep murmur reaches my ears that tends to reach the point of desperation. In that instant, as my anguish borders on a sudden vertigo, I'm able to perceive that the sound comes from some subtle point, remote and internal, beneath the everyday, and that it seems to carry the ominous hint of an imminent catastrophe and the warning of a cruel, tellurian rupture. And then that precise instant is invaded by a silence that quells all threats, a tense lucidity that assuages our fears, our confusions, our suspicions.

The first time I heard that murmur was many years ago. And a great deal of time passed before I heard it again. Or perhaps, immersed in hope, naivety or belief, I got used to ignoring it. Indifference can help you survive, it's true, but in the end it becomes a usurious debt that can never be paid back. And I'm not prepared to let that debt grow.

My desk is covered with photographs, documents, official reports, court transcripts, witness statements, audio recordings and videos that testify to the extreme cruelty that disturbed one summer night in a city in southern Mexico—a place that, due to a malicious intersection of events, destinies, serendipities and intentions, has become a symbol of the rule of the perverse under the guise of the normal: here is where global power and resistance collide.

It is a faithful portrait, in other words, of the world to come that we refuse to see, though it is already a reality in many places: the normalization of atrocity in the midst of formal politics, the empire of propaganda, the spectacle, the banality of telecommunications and the neutral tone of public discourse. We have stopped paying the price demanded by totalitarian societies and their inherent barbarism only to run the risks of globalized societies and the immanence of their barbarism.

The depraved will tends to unite dispersed negativity, making it once again possible for persons to be exterminated under the framework of institutional formalism. That murmur was an emanation from the great rift that annihilates everything human, a rift whose formation we refused to take seriously. The black wind: an immense and contagious effect, lethal and persistent; we can only understand it, sense it or evoke it with ideas, words, verses and specific music, like when Tom Waits sings, "*You gotta keep the devil way down in the hole / He's got the fire and the fury at his command...*" Evil is within the bounds of what we have accepted as normal: these are dark times. The concrete evil of abuse and injustice.

The tasks of the writer include that of sounding out the persistence of the perverse, which would prefer to remain invisible. The ideal of the free individual has culminated in the freedom to annihilate others in the space between the lines of the universal rules.

And atrocity occurs as if it were nothing. In the name of ideologies and institutions, human statutes are crushed. Evil has taken its place among us, sheltered by our faith in money, war and technique. Against all fictions, against the foulness of the cynics and the indifferent, we must refuse to become a part of it. I refuse to remain silent, to fall back on amnesia and contempt. Shouting is powerful, just as surviving means insisting on one's presence.

This story is being repeated around the world, but we refuse to see it. If anyone doubts or denies this, then I challenge them to finish this book.

Active reflection is a duty in the era of the ultra-capitalism of machines and its ever-expanding spiral.

My passion is one of clarification. I have based my work on the facts and I uphold the following prudent theses:

1. Nothing in these pages is fiction.
2. I believe in human rights and I defend the pro-persona principle in all of my work investigating and writing about the Iguala 43.
3. I am interested in offering the historical context needed to contemplate these events on a deeper level instead of falling into the trap of reducing everything to a simple clash between heroes and villains.
4. I contribute my own critical perspective, experiences or methods where pertinent.
5. I affirm that the Mexican government bears political and legal responsibility for the massacre in Iguala, and I support my position.
6. I argue that the same is true for the United States government and I give my reasons.
7. I reject the official investigation into the massacre as being inconsistent and incomplete.
8. I disbelieve those who detect fatalism or atavism in the phenomenon of violence in Mexico.
9. I document the historical, sociopolitical and material causes of violence in Mexico, as I have done in my previous books.

10. I describe how and why the 43 students and their classmates were exposed to extreme risks by their leaders.

When faced with the acceptance of horror, we must recover our lucidity and exercise our freedom to transform this tragic reality.

2

THE MASSACRE

On the night of September 26th, 2014, a group of students from the Ayotzinapa Rural Teachers' College traveled in two buses to the southern Mexican city of Iguala, Guerrero. When they reached the bus station, they *expropriated*, as was their custom, another three.[1]

Their plan was to return to the Ayotzinapa campus with these buses, which they would use to travel to Mexico City for the protest held each year on October 2nd to commemorate those killed at Tlatelolco Plaza during the 1968 student movement.

At 9:30 p.m., a group of police officers caught up to the vehicles and fired on the students, killing three. The police were able to cut them off again several blocks later and opened fire once more. Some of the students managed to escape and took refuge in nearby houses, while others tried to shield themselves with the buses.

At close to 11:00 p.m., a group of armed men on the outskirts of Iguala fired on a bus carrying the Chilpancingo Hornets soccer team, as well as on another car, resulting in the deaths of three more people. Another 25 were also wounded.

After both of these incidents, the official investigation states, 43 of the students were kidnapped, beaten and murdered by members of the criminal organization Guerreros Unidos with the complicity of the municipal police. Their bodies were burned that same night to destroy the evidence.

Weeks later, Mexican authorities found ashes and bones in a garbage dump located in the nearby town of Cocula, which in Nahuatl means "place of quarrels" or "place of undulations."

At the beginning of December 2014, a genetic analysis of the ashes conducted by Austria's University of Innsbruck positively identified one of the 43: Alexander Mora, 19 years old.

Among the 43, the case that most stands out is that of Julio César Mondragón Fontes, 22 years old. Terrified by the shots being fired at him and his companions, he ran off by himself, only to fall into the hands of the police. Another account states the opposite, that he stood his ground as the police fired on the students. His body appeared several hours later in an industrial zone of Iguala: he had been tortured, his eyes gouged out, the skin peeled from his face, dead from a skull fracture.

The state government, as well as that of the municipality in which the students were attacked, were in the hands of the Party of the Democratic Revolution (PRD). The federal government was controlled by members of the Institutional Revolution Party (PRI).

Federal authorities, who were aware of the night's events as they occurred, refused to intervene on the pretext of respecting local and state autonomy, even though they knew that the perpetrators had ties to organized crime.

Students and other witnesses have testified before the state prosecutor of Guerrero that federal police officers and soldiers from the 27th Infantry Battalion actively participated in the massacre. This contradicts the findings of the official investigation, which insists that the army and the federal police were mere witnesses to the events that night. A futile claim.

In general, crimes are committed by commission and omission. In this case, the soldiers, policemen and federal security officers who were present in Iguala that night—or giving orders to those who were—failed to act and are therefore responsible for the crimes of murder, torture and enforced disappearance committed on their watch.

On November 4th, 2014, the federal government announced the arrest of Iguala Mayor José Luis Abarca and his wife María de los Ángeles Pineda, along with a group of criminals and municipal police officers, for their alleged participation in these events.

In accordance with the Rome Statute of the International Criminal Court (1998), what happened that summer night in southern Mexico constitutes a crime against humanity that implicates Mexico's federal government as well as those of the state of Guerrero and the municipality where the aforementioned acts of barbarism occurred.[2]

In the paradox of our times, the massacre was consecrated before the world during an entertainment industry awards ceremony: in November 2014, during the Latin Grammys, René Pérez of the Puerto Rican reggaeton duo Calle 13 wore a black t-shirt with the legend "Ayotzinapa: Faltan 43" (Ayotzinapa: There's 43 Missing). To this image, which was seen around the world, the rapper added, "Tonight I'd like to talk to you about a struggle that's occurring in Mexico. We are all Ayotzinapa. We can't let this go on. Viva Mexico! Mexico, the country of impunity."[3]

As Octavio Paz wrote:

> Why?
> *Guilt is anger*
> *turned against itself:*
> *if*
> *an entire nation is ashamed*
> *it is a lion poised*
> *to leap.*[4]

3

TERRITORY IN RED

Ayotzinapa, which in Nahuatl means "river of baby squash" or "river of turtles," is a semi-tropical mountain town located some 400 kilometers south of Mexico City, on the outskirts of Tixtla and 125 kilometers from Iguala. It centers around the Raúl Isidro Burgos Rural Teachers' College, which was founded in 1926 as part of the nationwide educational crusade of the post-revolutionary epoch.[5] There are currently 245 teachers' colleges located throughout Mexico's 32 states, 17 of which are rural teachers' colleges. The legacy of a time that believed that education would ensure prosperity.

Construction began on the college's current campus in 1931. During this decade, the Ayotzinapa Rural Teachers' College solidified its nationalist ideology with ingredients taken from revolutionary Marxism, an ideology which endures to this day in the hearts of its professors and students and can even be seen on the school's walls, which are covered in colorful portraits of Ernesto "Che" Guevara ("I shall return and I will be millions"), Subcomandante Marcos ("We are dignity in rebellion"), Lucio Cabañas ("Protest is a right"). And warnings: "Ayotzinapa, the cradle of social consciousness," "If the government continues to repress and close rural teachers' colleges, the People will have the last word (Federation of Socialist Campesino Students of Mexico, FECSM)." Tenacity in rebellion.

I contemplate those students today as they march through the streets of the capital to protest their dead. They are the presence of a dispossession and a fury that would reclaim the life and unity of meaning that society has denied them. The steady gaze, the brilliant darkness of their eyes concentrates a malaise, a mineral sharpness. Their slogans are sad and exultant: they shake with a wounded incredulity. Experience and expectation offer a stinging contrast.

At the school in Ayotzinapa, the students live immersed in revolutionary slogans and are watched over by portraits of Marx, Engels, Lenin and Mao Zedong, whose lives and doctrines they study. Discipline and punishment for those who show weakness. The new students, the so-called skinheads, know this best. The colonial arches of the two-story building at the entrance give way to a more modern area where the classrooms and dormitories can be found.

There, dozens of students from Guerrero and elsewhere in Mexico squeeze together in bunk beds or on mattresses laid out on the ground. The school has 3.6 hectares of arable land and another 1.2 hectares that have been built up, of which only 35% are used for teaching. The rest, which border on farmland, house the students and teachers. Want unites the students with the land.

Clothing is hung out to dry on railings and the hallways echo with the daily activities of the students, who suffer from the shortages of a school that is out of favor with Mexico's educational authorities. Its conflict with the government has been a constant for decades. The state and federal governments tend to see the school as a subversive *foco* linked to revolutionary guerrillas: the red peril.

In Ayotzinapa, the phrases are repeated over and over in voices both sweet and admonishing, and the students express themselves with a tone of proclamation, conviction, denunciation and strident self-affirmation: "We want justice in Mexico," "We're disillusioned with the government," "Our rage is more than enough," "We miss our classmates, we want them back," "Government officials don't care about us," "The state needs to take responsibility," "They've lied to us, they've deceived us," "We demand justice, not amnesia,"

"We need to raise our voices," "Don't trust them," "Enough promises," "The state is paving the path of violence," "Discontent is spreading," "It was the state."

And, especially, "They were taken alive, we want them back alive!"

Guerrero is the second poorest state in Mexico, as the Mexican government itself recognizes, with close to 71% of the population living below the poverty level.[6] Guerrero is divided into 81 municipalities and seven regions: Acapulco, Centro, Norte, Tierra Caliente, Costa Chica, Costa Grande and La Montaña. Its geomorphology is uneven, as both the Sierra Madre del Sur and the Sierra del Norte cross the state. Its principal economic activities are agriculture (corn, sorghum, rice, limes, coffee, watermelons), tourism (the beach resorts of Acapulco and Ixtapa-Zihuatanejo and, more inland, Taxco) and mining (gold, silver, copper, iron...).[7]

The state is named after Vicente Guerrero, a hero of the Mexican War of Independence (1810–1821) who was born in Tixtla.[8] In 1821, Vicente Guerrero signed a pact with the Spanish Royal Army, headed by Agustín de Iturbide, which ratified Mexico's independence, recognized the monarchy of Fernando VII, established Catholicism as the country's sole religion and called for unity between all social classes.

With the support of the Liberal Party, Vicente Guerrero became the president of Mexico in 1829. Among other initiatives, he promoted religious tolerance, education, the arts, industry, science and trade. And he issued the decree that abolished slavery throughout the country. This measure earned him the animosity of U.S. slaveowners.

In 1831, Vicente Guerrero was betrayed by his conservative opponents and executed in Oaxaca. Traces of blood and rebellion have been present in Guerrero since the pre-Hispanic era, when the Yope tribe resisted the Aztecs, never submitting to their rule. During the conquest and subsequent colonization, the Spaniards exterminated the Yopes and the insurrectionary impulse took root in the heart of the region's mestizo communities, subject to the domination of caciques and the premodern mentality or by authoritarian politics, in which disagreements tend to be settled by force.[9] The law of the machete or the gun.

Omens: When I heard about the massacre in Iguala, I had just finished working on a study for an academic organization that analyzed youth and the threat of crime in Mexico and Latin America as a whole. My conclusions were scathing: I observed that government institutions tend to impose policies centering on repression while largely ignoring prevention (even though they claim that this is one

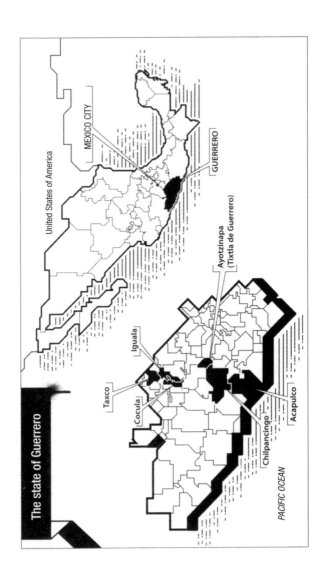

The state of Guerrero

United States of America

MEXICO CITY

GUERRERO

Ayotzinapa
(Tixtla de Guerrero)

Iguala

Taxco

Cocula

Chilpancingo

Acapulco

PACIFIC OCEAN

of their aims), just as they avoid disciplinary reflections from the perspective of criminal law and an understanding of crime as a phenomenon.

It's disconcerting that hurried and authoritarian actions, which tend towards illegality, are what mark the public presence of the government. From this authoritarian point of view, problems should be "fixed" with unprecedented promptness. This is applauded by many, even though, as in the case of Ayotzinapa, the preliminary investigations may be unsound from a legal perspective. The victims aren't even conceded the minimum justice guaranteed under the law by their existence in society.

I have insisted that damage control (carried out through press releases, radio, television and social media) is more important for the government than ensuring that justice is done and that the country's laws and institutions are respected.

As always, my arguments are backed up with data and, of the available data, I prefer negative information because it shows the greatest contrasts. I agree with those who believe that discouraging statistics promote progress because they force us to detect and hopefully resolve anomalies and failures.

I have a reputation for prophesying evils that, to the misfortune of all, tend to come to pass, as occurred nearly 20 years ago, when I predicted the decay that would spread to every corner of the country.[10] In the midst of jubilant reformism, few wanted to deeply examine reality or the working of our institutions.

It used to be thought, and still is in some parts, that sounding the alarm was a trade for spoilsports, activists, radicals, the bitter and resentful. People are used to understanding life as entertainment or as a game played by conflicting interests. Those of us who hold the opposite point of view, that of listening to the victims, are not deluded. The complacency of focusing on the *positive* only benefits the constituted order, which wishes to reproduce itself without accepting meaningful change.

The average age in Mexico City is estimated to be between 29 and 30. When I was that age, the Sex Pistols were shouting *No Future!*—a generational slogan that buried the dreams of young people in industrial societies on the threshold of the postindustrial world of financial globalization, the war machine, the predatory economy of free markets and self-regulation.

This combination of policies has condemned young people in Mexico and throughout the Americas, Europe, Asia and Africa to a sort of *juvencide*. Something worse than the lack of a future. When I got my start as a writer, I was playing in my brother Pablo's rock group Enigma! One of my first texts was an interview with a gang of marginalized kids who called themselves Los Mierdas Punk. One of their anthems was our song

Cucaracha, a song in which they saw a reflection of themselves, a song whose lyrics dealt ironically with society's disdain for the marginalized populations living in the suburbs of that epoch.

Los Mierdas Punk: publishing that name in the midst of a conservative society and recording the furious and heartbreaking testimonies of young people who were lost in the cruelest of times was the smallest contribution I could make. It's a challenge that I've tried to live up to.

Between the country of that article and the country of today, a troubling horizon appears: there were then 70 million people living in Mexico. Now there are 121 million and in another decade there will be 130 million. Of Mexico's over 16 million young people, half are in poverty. And the problem will only get worse: half of all Mexicans are younger than 26 and there are fewer boys than girls, who endure discrimination and constant aggressions: most of them are victims of some type of violence, inequality, discrimination or abuse. These figures surpass the world average.

For someone like me, who grew up under the banner of a generation that fought for a better world, the present is unacceptable. Aside from a small minority, young people are strangers in their own land—instead of being given the opportunities they need in terms of education, work, culture, justice and civility, they fall victim to violence, crime, drug addiction, the informal economy, gangsterism, guns and industrial and sexual exploitation.

They also confront the possibility of self-destruction. Young people face the dilemma of legality or illegality, as the ballot as an instrument of political participation or change has a precarious place under the shadow of a new authoritarianism concealed by three pillars: a formal democracy that is nevertheless blind to substance, which keeps reforms proposed outside the system from being properly debated and openly promotes counter-reforms; the habitual tendency to turn to states of exception as a tool of governance; and the legitimation provided by the monopolistic powers of the mass media, which dominates the public discourse through the uniformity of the official story and the propaganda of "positive perceptions," while social networks conform themselves with being a safety valve of old-fashioned ochlocracy: government by the mob, as the dictionary defines the term, but reduced to a limited number of characters on a screen interconnected with the virtual world.

The issue at hand goes beyond the ideological-partisan sphere: it's a call for ethics and responsibility on the part of those who should be upholding them. In every country of the world, the extermination of young people, in one way or another, has become our expectation of what will soon be habitual. The *juvenicide* begins either with an attack on the university or its total destruction. *Universitas*: the field of egalitarian aspirations falls victim to technified barbarism. Its surrogates are violence, hedonism, exploitation and obligatory consumption...

Among some worker-campesino sectors with ties to the Communist Party, the popularity of Marxism-Leninism in Latin America following the triumph of the Cuban Revolution in 1959 led to a great deal of enthusiasm for the creation of a popular revolutionary movement that would oppose the presidential authoritarianism and one-party state of the PRI.[11]

Such was the case of Lucio Cabañas, a graduate from the Ayotzinapa Rural Teachers' College, a former member of the Communist Youth and the grandson of a revolutionary who fought with Emiliano Zapata. A one-time student leader in the FECSM, he got a teaching job in Atoyac and took it on himself to raise the social consciousness of the town's residents. This earned him the enmity of the local powers that be. In 1967, police opened fire on a peaceful demonstration that he had organized to ask for the resignation of a principal who, under pressure from local caciques, had been harassing the parents of the school's students. The massacre exacerbated grievances that were already ancestral.

A dozen casualties, including a pregnant woman, decided the fate of Lucio Cabañas: from then on he would be a clandestine militant, taking refuge in the mountains of Guerrero, indoctrinating townspeople and farmworkers (through his Party of the Poor) and punishing caciques and the rich (through his Justice Brigade). The government's contempt only aggravated the situation.

In 1974, the guerrilla leader kidnapped the PRI's candidate for governor, who was later rescued by the police. He was killed several months later during a shootout with the Mexican Army. And so Lucio Cabañas became a revolutionary icon in Guerrero: in the name of his ideals, he had nothing to lose but his life.

Genaro Vázquez, another social militant who graduated from the Ayotzinapa Rural Teachers' College, met a similar fate. The founder of the Independent Campesino Center (CCI) and an opponent of the regime during the 1950s, official intolerance radicalized his political struggle. After the government imprisoned him, his comrades in the National Revolutionary Civic Association (ACNR) broke him out.

Once freed, he led a guerrilla movement in the mountains of Guerrero. As the military was pursuing him down a highway in Michoacán, Genaro Vázquez's car crashed. It seems that he was only wounded but was then executed by the soldiers. The specter of guerrilla warfare began to haunt these territories.

In revolutionary ideology, sacrificial blood is an event that gives rise to a continuous struggle, as would be repeated in 1994 by Subcomandante Marcos, the leader of the neo-indigenist movement of the Zapatista National Liberation Army (EZLN) (1994–2000): "We, the same dead as always, have come here today to tell our dead that we are ready, that the long night of lies that refuses to end needs more blood to fertilize the seed that will grow into the light of tomorrow. We have come here to speak to our dead."[12] The future is written in blood, in what is called dignified rage.

And, in many parts of the world, solidarity with the poor.

4

THE VIOLENT CYCLE

Insurrection against the established order has been a constant act of faith in Guerrero over the past five decades. Marxism-Leninism has reasserted itself in rural areas, leading to the emergence of a variety of insurgent groups—a product of the revolutionary idea of forming people's armies to oppose a country's official armed forces.

The People's Union was founded at the Autonomous University of Chilpancingo (UACH) in the state capital during the epoch of Cabañas and Vázquez. This organization would later form the basis for the Revolutionary Clandestine Workers' and People's Union Party (PROCUP) in 1971.

In 1996, the Democratic Revolutionary Tendency-People's Army (TDR-EP) emerged in Guerrero, while the Popular Revolutionary Army (EPR) announced its formation in Guerrero and Oaxaca. A split in the latter group produced the

Revolutionary Army of the Insurgent People (ERPI) in 1997–1998. The Villista Revolutionary Army of the People (EVRP) split off from the EPR in 1999.

Despite their differences in principles, strategies and tactics, these movements are characterized by their revolutionary potency and their war on the established powers in Mexico and around the world. Absolute fervor for revolutionary sacrifice.

Other subversive groups have emerged in Mexico in recent years, such as the Revolutionary Armed Forces of the People (FARP, 2000) and the May 23rd Jaramillista Commando of Morelos (CJM, 2004). If the guerrilla organizations mentioned here are only a fraction of those formed in Mexico in the 20th and 21st Centuries, they stand out because of their theater of operations: Guerrero, Morelos, Michoacán, Oaxaca and Chiapas, with isolated actions elsewhere, such as in Mexico City.

What unites them? I have an answer to this decisive question: in the ideological substratum of these groups, as in the ideology taught to the students of the Ayotzinapa Rural Teachers' College, the concept of popular sovereignty prevails as an organizational focus and a call to action.

To understand how the ideas and praxis of the Ayotzinapa students are connected to those of other revolutionary groups, it needs to be understood that the central committee of the Raúl Isidro

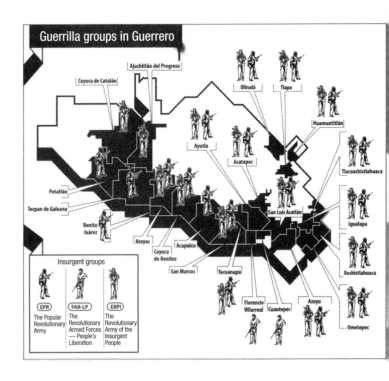

Burgos Teachers' College Student Association is organically linked with the FECSM. Founded in 1935 and currently active at 35 rural teachers' colleges across the country, the FECSM's "principal objective has been, since its founding, to educate the children of campesinos and to defend the rights of the people, following the Marxist-Leninist line."[13] Each school with a FECSM presence has a Political and Ideological Orientation Committee (COPI), through which the FECSM maintains contact with "a semi-clandestine student organization with a nationwide presence, made up of students at Mexico's rural teachers' colleges." The Executive Student Committee, the Struggle Committee and the Political and Ideological Orientation Committee at the Ayotzinapa Rural Teachers' College would have been the ones responsible for "commissioning" the students' actions in Iguala on September 26th, 2014.

The importance of the concept of popular sovereignty for these organizations can be seen in the first thesis of the ERPI's manifesto, which states: "We feel that revolutionary change in Mexico will be the product of many divergent efforts and that, in the struggle for change, there are many trenches in which one can fight. None can claim to have a patent certifying themselves as the only true revolutionaries, nor can they, out of pride and contempt for others, attempt to hegemonize the struggle and assume a leading role. Those who think and act in such a manner are perhaps the least revolutionary of all, if we can speak of these categories in such a way. We therefore recognize that revolutionaries have a commitment to the people and not to individuals or organizations."[14]

The ERPI manifesto then states: "We therefore accept and try to live up to the example set by Vicente Guerrero when he said 'My fatherland comes first.' By acting in accordance with this conviction, we feel that no personal or group commitments are more important to the popular struggle currently underway than our commitment to the people and that our participation in the revolutionary struggle only makes sense because we fight for the people, we fight with the people and we form part of the people." The people, the fatherland, the purity of the revolutionary will.

By exalting popular sovereignty, the responsibility for decisions and actions falls on the shoulders of the agents of popular sovereignty and their organizations. Legitimacy is determined by their faithfulness (or lack thereof) to said sovereignty, which in turn sanctions the agents themselves. The closed circle of faith.

This implies, in other words, a domination of one's self, or autarchy (from the Greek αὐταρχία, "absolute power"). In consequence, each action preliminary to the revolutionary event embodies the revolution and legitimates itself *ipso facto* by looking to the present and future, in which the blood of the combatants who came before will serve as the essential "fertilizer" for the revolution, a fertilizer that should be used continuously until its coming.

I can recall the teachings of Ernesto "Che" Guevara on the subject: "Each and every one of us readily pays his or her quota of sacrifice, conscious of being rewarded with the satisfaction of fulfilling a duty, conscious of advancing with everyone toward the New Man glimpsed on the horizon."[15] The coming of the end and the beginning of time.

In Mexico, the intellectual synthesis of popular sovereignty and absolute revolutionary power isn't just found among guerrilla groups, but also represents a common ethic for the worker-campesino militants of the far left and social justice activists, particularly those dissident teachers who oppose the official union, such as those belonging to the State Coordinator of Education Workers of Guerrero (CETEG).

The activism of this organization is analogous to that of Oaxaca's Section XXII of the National Education Workers' Union / National Coordinator of Education Workers (SNTE/CNTE): its extremism is instrumental, whether fighting to implement a political program or negotiating a budget with the government.

These leftist-revolutionary groupings—which have connections with human rights workers, non-governmental organizations and others who support them for ideological reasons, such as lawyers, academics, journalists, indigenists, etc.—communicate the everyday relevance of this synthesis to the rural and urban communities in which they are based. Upon entering the coercive-repressive dynamic of the state, they tend to increasingly radicalize their actions, objectives and goals under the directive to capitalize on any and all crises with the goal of accelerating and consummating the revolutionary event. Mobilizations feed on growing or cyclical exasperation.

This revolutionary cosmovision determines the actions of students, teachers and militants. Whether these actions are passive (such as civil disobedience or peaceful resistance) or active (protests and rallies; blockades of streets, avenues, bridges and highways; the requisition of money, gasoline, vehicles and merchandise; vandalism of government buildings, private businesses and the offices of multinational corporations), the goal is to make plain the failure of the established order and spread the rebellion to other groups or sectors.

The government's ineptitude, corruption, inefficiency and ineffectiveness play into their hands.

I can recall an episode that occurred in 2011, when students from Ayotzinapa held a protest in

Chilpancingo and blocked the highway. There was a confrontation with the police, who fired on the demonstrators after seeing them attack a nearby gas station: two students died. One gas station employee later died from the burns he received while trying to prevent an explosion when one of the students tried to burn the place down.[16] Only from an irrational point of view can one threaten people's lives and justify it with an ideological defense. Leaders ask why this episode was never clarified by the authorities. Likewise, why could they never foresee the risks for students in Chilpancingo and Iguala?

The father of one of the 43 has stated that, when the time comes, he will denounce the student leaders who encouraged his sons to take the risks that led him to his death. It's the least he can do for the memory of his son and his fellow victims. I am convinced that the perfect complement to normalized barbarism can be found in those who exacerbate it in the name of a better future.

At the Ayotzinapa Rural Teachers' College, there is an area that is under the exclusive control of these leaders: a zone restricted to the initiated. The clandestine network that drives revolutionary activism in Guerrero.[17] From the perspective of revolutionary ideology, the 43 students are victims offered up by their leaders in a utilitarian sacrifice.

Comrade Duch (Kaing Guek Eav), warden of the infamous S-21 prison under the Khmer Rouge, has always denied the cruelty of his actions and those of his subordinates: "Malice and cruelty formed no part of our ideology. The ideology was in command. My men put the ideology into practice." During his time, there were 20,000 mass graves and over 1.7 million victims. His words are a forever-pertinent warning, the equivalent of the categorical imperative used by the Nazis to justify their genocide.[18]

This aspect also recalls the nexus between politics and crime: one of the most significant and self-legitimizing activities for Mexico's guerrillas has been kidnapping.[19] A variety of revolutionary groups have been committing high-profile kidnappings since the 1970s to finance their activities or conduct prisoner exchanges. Groups such as PROCUP intensified their reliance on kidnapping during the 1990s, as did criminal organizations.

In 1994, the EZLN kidnapped the governor of Chiapas and the EPR kidnapped an important banker. In Guerrero, kidnapping would become one of the primary activities of both guerrillas and gangsters.

In recent years, the Mexican government has detected a sort of anti-institutional synergy among gangs, drug traffickers and revolutionary groups. The director of the Ayotzinapa Rural Teachers'

College has declared that the school's campus is open to students, workers, visitors and all Tixtla residents, who come to exercise in the afternoons, "but delinquents aren't allowed here." From the government's point of view, this synergy determines Guerrero's destabilization, chaos, insecurity and violence. Under these conditions, any dissidence is interpreted as a criminal act, something excessive.[20]

What's unacceptable is the lack of respect for the rights of others, among them journalists, who are harassed by criminals, leftist activists and the government in Guerrero.[21]

Two years ago, I attended a university colloquium. Current affairs were being discussed and I wanted to bring up something that has been ignored by the academy: the social contract of the nation-state, the rule of law. How can something that is increasingly non-existent continue to be recognized? Nobody responded, even though I was addressing all participants. Faced with their silence, I added that the definitive emigration of a country's citizens should be used as an index by which to judge societies. Ours would fail.

Between 1990 and 1993, 68.5% of the immigrants from Guerrero—together with those from Chiapas, Oaxaca and Veracruz—traveled to the United States without a visa, a figure that rose to 92.8% in the period between 2001 and 2005. The compulsory movement of these immigrants suggests the hopelessness of their lived reality. Among all the regions of Mexico, Guerrero tops the list of those whose residents travel to the United States and never come back.[22]

Halfway through the second decade of the 21st Century, 13% of the population of Guerrero lives in the United States. The cause of migration is not so much poverty as profound dissatisfaction, accentuated by social tensions.

In 2013, another guerrilla organization emerged in Guerrero: the Revolutionary Armed Forces—People's Liberation (FAR-LP), which proclaimed in a 2014 communiqué: "To all our brothers in the struggle, let us prepare to advance from strategic defense to a generalized offensive against the state. You know what measures need to be taken; we cannot let this moment pass us by, we must do it for our dead brothers, it's time to put into practice the slogan of Fatherland or Death."[23] Once again, the sacrificial imperative and the vigilante impulse intertwine in a call to insurrection.

On October 9th, 2014, the ERPI announced the creation of the September 26th Justice Brigade, which would fight the criminal organization Guerreros Unidos in solidarity with the disappeared students from Ayotzinapa.[24] The violent cycle has its future guaranteed.

Whenever I visit Iguala and Chilpancingo, almost nobody expresses the outrage breathed in Ayotzinapa over the fate of the 43. Nor do the locals adopt any of the slogans condemning the Mexican state, even though they too disapprove of the actions of the federal and state governments: most Guerrero residents feel that the mobilizations for the disappeared students are organized by people unconnected to the tragedy.[25]

In both cities, you can feel a certain weariness with the daily excesses of both criminal organizations and the students and their support brigades.

In the name of "contributions to the cause," Ayotzinapa students and other activist groups often block the free circulation of vehicles and pedestrians, expropriate vehicles and other goods, deprive people of their freedom, damage the property of others, vandalize buildings, exact money or donations in kind and threaten to use violence if their demands go unmet. Or they bear firearms, justifying themselves by saying that it's one thing to have weapons to support the cause and another to be an armed organization. Ideology provides them with their rhetoric and their subterfuges.

This has been going on in Guerrero for some time now, but the situation has intensified since 2014. For some of the state's residents, that night of atrocity in Iguala resembled the criminal dynamics between two gangs more than it did a political struggle.

As we walk down the streets of Iguala, a construction industry executive who has been both victim and witness to the disorder in Guerrero warns me about the "falcons," those spies for criminal organizations that circulate through town on noisy scooters or sit next to people as they eat lunch. They're everywhere. And he tells me that "the students should know that the crimes, misdemeanors and violations of constitutional principles that they're committing are aggravated when committed by a group, as the Federal Organized Crime Law establishes that when three or more people organize to permanently or repeatedly undertake actions that, on their own or combined with other actions, have the goal or end result of committing the crimes of assault, theft or kidnapping, then, for this alone, they will receive the same punishment as members of criminal organizations."

I lift up my eyes to the avenue encircling Iguala, watching vehicles circulate in an environment where it reaches 95° by midday: the city, in the shadow of rugged mountains and vegetation that is green and bountiful in the rainy season but is now yellow and dry, is a cauldron of iniquity, want, chaos, criminal opulence. And, of course, of work, resistance and honor on the part of many of its citizens.

The construction industry executive goes on: "I know that they, the leftist activists, don't respect the law on the pretext of their ideology, but the rest of us do want to respect it. And it's not right for them to attack us—the worst part is that they're putting themselves on the same level as the criminals and police officers who murdered their classmates." He asks: "Why did the parents of these students allow their children to break the law instead of studying, why did the school's director give them his blessing? The student committee and their leaders are also to blame and nobody has asked them to be held accountable, they're taking advantage of their dead." Who is he referring to?

Leftist activists and their supporters tend to pass over certain decisive facts in order to better support the cause of the 43, but it's worth mentioning what they omit. According to publicly available figures, for example, the students have taken between 30 and 80 million pesos from toll booths and have "expropriated" over 120 privately owned and government vehicles, worth close to 30 million pesos.[26] Impunity also persists among dissidents. The relationship between those who handle money for the cause and their followers is just as asymmetrical as the inequality in Guerrero. "The leaders give the families of the 43 a mere 2,000 pesos," our executive emphasizes.

The parents of the 43, he explains, "are the ones who should be the most sensitive to this situation, because when they sent their children to the Ayotzinapa Rural Teachers' College, they thought they were giving them a better future, not the opposite: danger, abuse, manipulation at the hands of their leaders, death…" An issue that tends to be avoided.

Over time, leftist ideology has adopted a dogma: whoever criticizes the cause only helps the right. The specter of Joseph Stalin haunts these words, yet this attitude is more generalized than one might think, although it is necessary to make distinctions.

Among the activists in favor of the 43, an anarchist line has taken hold that has only intensified the revolutionary tradition. This particular anarchist tendency considers itself to be flexible/informal and has as its aim "the immediate destruction of capital and the state" by any means at its disposal. It brings nihilists together with a variety of revolutionaries and other groups and individuals that oppose the sociopolitical system and civilization as a whole. It allows for secessionism or autonomous government and there are those who advocate for the immediate formation of an Autonomous Territory of the South, encompassing Guerrero, Michoacán, Oaxaca and Chiapas, to be created through war, chaos, destabilization and social polarization.

One of the activists belonging to this tendency declared in 2012: "We could push for the physical elimination of the candidate of the so-called 'progressive movement' (Andrés Manuel López Obrador) with the clear intention of provoking his followers to action and bringing about a 'generalized insurrection.' We anarchists would then have a lot to do, not because we foresee 'revolutionary possibilities' nor because we place our hopes in the much-hyped 'changes' or 'transformations' of social democracy, but because we would have the marvelous opportunity to spread chaos and bring about those ephemeral moments in which anarchism comes to life."[27]

This activist, who is believed to have inspired the arson attack on Mexico's National Palace in 2014, was declared to be *persona non grata* in the EZLN-held territory in Chiapas during the 1990s and was deported from Cuba, whose government accused him of being a subversive agent of the United States government. In Mexico's anarchist movement, he is considered to be an *agent provocateur* in the employ of the Central Intelligence Agency (CIA) and he was deported to the United States by Mexican authorities in January 2014. In his case file, manipulated destruction and the management of domestic conflicts for geopolitical motives converge.

In 2013, I was invited to a literary festival in Bilbao. Upon arriving at the airport, I discovered that the airline had lost my suitcase. I had to report the loss and this took time. The taxi they had sent for me had already gone on its way. I took another without exactly knowing where I was going. I asked the driver to take me to a hotel; I only told him one word, which echoed in my memory and which I must have read in a message from one of the organizers: *silk*.

The driver took me to a hotel with a similar name. It was the right one. I could barely sleep that night, something nearby was vibrating. Perhaps it was the echo of Berlin: I had just come from the sometimes rainy, sometimes sunny German capital. The hotel I had stayed at was near the ultramodern Berlin Hauptbahnhof and a power station. I am sensitive to these types of influences and insomnia kept me from resting for four or five days.

As I was eating breakfast on the hotel terrace, I discovered the true cause of the subtle vibrations that had kept me awake: I was across the street from Frank Gehry's Guggenheim Bilbao. A brilliant construction of twisted, curvilinear titanium plates, glass and limestone that the architect seems to have extracted from the mind of some cosmic can opener.

From intuition I moved to observation: I spent the next three days contemplating the building, trying to understand it. The architect's artificial contribution to the surrounding environment shaped its telluric density. I believe that the creative labor here went beyond that of designing a museum: the building is a commutator of energy that completely transformed the city of Bilbao.

When the museum was built, the surrounding area was abandoned, little more than a grouping of ancient industrial facilities that recalled a time of rage, clenched teeth and horror that had been long since overcome. On the third day, after circling the gigantic building and observing it from different vantage points, I decided to enjoy it from the inside. My visit was a memorable event; it satisfied my fascination with labyrinths.

Inside the museum, in a hallway on the third floor, I located the heart of the museum: a point at which the entire structure of the building seemed to tremble under my feet. The sensation was shocking, electromagnetic, savage: it was as if I had come in contact with the building's sacred spot. I quickly fled, my pulse racing, frightened by the certainty that I could have destroyed the building with a precise blow to this spot, its invisible fulcrum.

I had intuited and observed the secret of the museum, the intersection that revealed its energy. The concept of energy I'm referring to here does not only involve energy existing in a medium or physical environment, like that caused by electro-magnetic waves which are directly transmitted without displacing the conducting material, but also the "mnemonic waves" of history and culture that echo into the present.

As Georges Didi-Huberman has said, waves of memory traverse and affect an element: a culture in its history, which is not completely fluid, and so there are tensions, resistances, symptoms, crises, ruptures, catastrophes.[28] An underlying chord that echoes down the years, without end.

Something similar happens to me with every-thing I investigate. Approaching a reality in order to understand it demands that we examine the information it generates and submit it to a scrutiny that tells us what we want to know, forwards and backwards. What is the game behind the game of the massacre of the 43?

5

ENDLESS GRIEVANCES

For decades, but especially during the 1970s, the military's human rights violations (illegal arrests, beatings, torture, rapes, disappearances, executions) have weighed on Guerrero's collective life, helping turn the state's social consciousness in an anti-institutional direction, opposing the armed forces, the police and the political system as a whole. The anger provoked by injustice tends not to be slight.

The Mexican Army has been loyal to the country's institutions, as we can see from its history. And 403 soldiers fell during the war on drug trafficking (2007–2012).[29] Its contributions to civic life have been invaluable during natural disasters and other emergencies. But, according to the National Human Rights Commission (CNDH), the dirty war against guerrillas and leftist militants in Guerrero—an integral part of the Mexican Army's war on drugs—has included the executions of at least 250 people and the disappearance of another 531 more.[30]

A former public prosecutor and interior secretary for the state of Guerrero has stated that, during the 1970s, "airplanes took off from the Pie de la Cuesta Air Force Base and threw cadavers and live prisoners into the sea."[31] Among the many theories that have circulated regarding the disappearance of the 43, there is one arguing that they met a similar fate.

On August 25th, 1974, for example, an activist named Rosendo Radilla Pacheco was stopped at a military checkpoint. The last place he was seen alive was the army barracks in Atoyac de Álvarez, Guerrero. No one ever heard from him again.[32] The victim's family reported his disappearance, and in 2001, the CNDH urged the government to act.

When the CNDH's recommendation was met by silence, the family took the case before the Inter-American Commission on Human Rights (IACHR) on November 15th, 2001. The IACHR ordered the Mexican government to follow the recommendations that had been issued by the CNDH. When the government refused to act, the IACHR referred the case to the Inter-American Court of Human Rights.

The court issued its ruling on November 23rd, 2009, condemning the Mexican government for serious human rights violations. In the wake of this incident, the Supreme Court established that the rulings of the Inter-American Court of Human Rights are binding and that Mexico's judges must treat all human rights treaties as the law of the land.

Another important effect of the Radilla ruling was that soldiers accused of human rights violations can no longer be judged by military tribunals; their cases must now be turned over to civilian courts.

Disappearances that are the work of criminal organizations and disappearances carried out by soldiers, marines or police officers are both consequences of the drug war initiated by the Mexican government, in which the number of victims fluctuates between 70,000 dead and 20,000 disappeared (according to official figures) and 120,000 dead and disappeared (according to independent estimates).[33] The great ossuary that the government insists on denying, against all rational principles.

Now, as I write these lines, underground rock echoes in my ears and I think of its unconquered legions: those whose lives don't matter. There's a line by Alfonso Reyes, falling somewhere between curiosity and astonishment, about how 12,000 people disappear each year and nobody knows what happens to them. They seem to leave by a secret door or enter some oblique plane that erases them from the everyday.

More than half a century after these words were written, we know that, for example, close to 14,000 people disappear each year in Spain alone. In Chile, 50,000 people disappear annually and, in Mexico, someone has disappeared every two hours since 2012: on average, 13 people disappear every day in our country.[34] How can we accept the tragedy of the disappeared?

To refer to those killed on the battlefield, Léon Bloy coined a phrase: the flock of souls, the sheep of eternity that will perhaps be redeemed by the Final Judgement. In our desacralized, profane, secular, lay age, it seems inappropriate to use this phrase. Military terminology has supplied us with a crude and impersonal insult whose neutrality was designed for bureaucratic calculations: *casualty*, used to refer to soldiers who have been killed, captured or otherwise rendered unfit for active duty.

When used in non-military situations, such as accident reports, the word *casualty* generally applies to a person who is dead or wounded. The original use of this term has no place in the world of today, as it referred to chance, luck and fortune, as death was understood in the medieval era.

The tolerated extermination of persons under ultracapitalism—which encompasses those killed by wars, pandemics and the effects of natural catastrophes caused by climate change and the plunder of the natural world, those exploited by criminal organizations and their illegal industries (such as the trafficking of women and children) and those exploited by industries paying miserable wages—has led to the generalization of another term of military origin, which is flaunted left and right: *collateral damage*, which refers to the "unintentional" or "accidental" damage caused by military operations.

This term was coined during the Vietnam War and also refers to shooting or bombing errors that damage one's own territories or those of allies: friendly fire. *Collateral damage* is a term that arose from the Harvard Business School and its criteria of effectiveness, efficiency, productivity and optimization of results.[35]

While speaking with a friend who has been an analyst of the Mexican presidency for some decades now, we recall that when our politicians went off to study in elite U.S. universities, they brought many ideas back with them to reform our country.

In the academic sphere, in political magazines, in intellectual coteries or simply in dinners with friends, a familiar thesis was repeated and then finally proclaimed by a presidential candidate at the end of the 1980s: what Mexico needed was a war, like those waged by the United States.

Unfortunately, the governing classes of both countries reached an agreement in 2005 to unleash a war on drug trafficking south of the U.S. border. The thousands of victims of that decision, which had been gestating for some time, express the new understanding of global governance: the collateral and the additional are subordinated to actions undertaken with foreseen risks that are accepted with almost no oversight. The secondary, which lacks convergent importance for the management plan, is condemned to be cast aside. Those executed, those killed "by accident," those disappeared for one reason or another: all vile numbers that invisibilize their fate. The negative emanation that we discovered too late.

Mexico's authorities tend to offer questionable numbers on disappearances: in May 2014, the Interior Secretariat reported that there had been 8,000 disappearances in Mexico, a figure, it was said, that was determined by analyzing and purging the previous figure of 27,000. In June, another figure was offered: there had been 16,000 disappearances.

The CNDH, in turn, had issued a report months beforehand stating that the number of people who had disappeared in Mexico was 27,243. All of these numbers were lower than the ones that had come before. The method used to purge the list of disappearances was clearly contradictory and inconsistent.[36]

The government has baselessly defended its data: it only counts what state or federal authorities "document without discrepancies." Figures drawn up at a desk, avoiding the facts.

Returning to the massacre: in Guerrero, between Iguala, Cocula and Taxco, there is a "corridor" of disappearances and clandestine graves, which tells us that the barbarism of Ayotzinapa is far from exceptional.[37] In 2010, 55 bodies were found in a ventilation shaft of Taxco's La Concha mine. In May of that same year, a group of soldiers disappeared six people; in May 2013, 14 people were kidnapped by armed men and 33 buried skeletons were found; that July, another 17 people were taken away by force; 17 bodies were found in February 2014, seven that April and another nine in May; 76 unknown persons and four skeletal remains were buried in the Iguala municipal cemetery between 2013 and 2014, a period that corresponds to the mayoralty of Abarca, whom the authorities accuse of being responsible for the disappearance of the 43.

As David Huerta has written:

> We bite into the shadow
> And in the shadow
> The dead appear
> Like lamps and fruit
> Like glasses of blood
> Like stones from the abyss…[38]

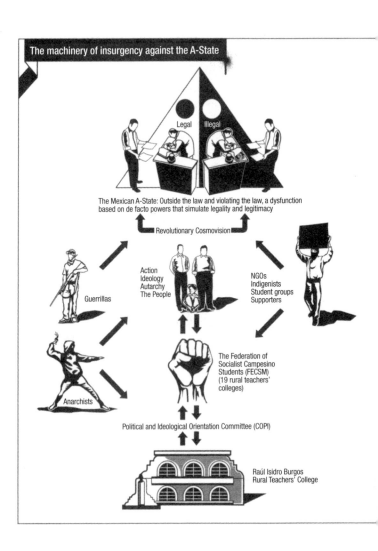

The machinery of insurgency against the A-State

Legal   Illegal

The Mexican A-State: Outside the law and violating the law, a dysfunction based on de facto powers that simulate legality and legitimacy

Revolutionary Cosmovision

Guerrillas

Action
Ideology
Autarchy
The People

NGOs
Indigenists
Student groups
Supporters

Anarchists

The Federation of Socialist Campesino Students (FECSM) (19 rural teachers' colleges)

Political and Ideological Orientation Committee (COPI)

Raúl Isidro Burgos Rural Teachers' College

6

NUMBERS THAT ARE PEOPLE

I have occasionally been asked why, instead of collecting facts, going through the archives and comparing different perspectives, I don't simply illustrate the available testimony and let the witnesses speak. I have said before, and it is worth repeating now, that with testimony there's always a certain impossibility to testify.[39] A witness only ever understands one part of the situation they've lived through, while the survivors are burdened with the silence of those who have died.

As Giorgio Agamben has said, this is where the problem of historical knowledge lies: the non-coincidence between facts and truth, between verification and comprehension. I must therefore commit myself to go further in order to try and comprehend.

A non-governmental organization has recorded 460 reports of disappearances and around 500 murders in that zone of Guerrero.[40] Killing and disappearing people has become a custom. This deeply-rooted violence determines the lack of testimony and describes an everyday atmosphere of horror, grievance, despondency, darkness.

Among the documents in my possession, there is one that has revealed much on the violent situation in southern Mexico: in 2013, the five most violent municipalities in the country were all located in Guerrero; the following year, Acapulco came in second place nationwide, surpassed only by Oaxaca.[41] Guerrero also leads the country in terms of violence against women.[42]

In historic terms, this document tells us that Mexico's homicide rate declined from 1940 on, reaching its lowest point in 2007. From 2008 on, it begins to recover. In Guerrero, this decline was slower than in the rest of the country: the state had the highest homicide rate in the country between 1979 and 2001, on average 143% higher than the national rate. In 2012, it was 238% higher.[43]

Each time I read figures that stand for violence and death, I make an effort to balance my conflicting emotions: how can we let people's lives end up as a list of facts, as graphs, as spreadsheets that will only be replaced by others? The darkness of numbers, the glory of each victim.

And the repetition of mourning: while Guerrero's homicide rate was the highest in the country between 1979 and 2001, it was not during the period between 2002 and 2005, but was once again in 2006 and 2007. Between 2008 and 2011, Guerrero's homicide rate was surpassed by that of Chihuahua, a state whose level of violence was unprecedented for Mexico. In 2013, Guerrero reclaimed the top position.

According to this document, the motives for homicide in Guerrero in the period between 1979 and 2013 were interpersonal conflicts; organized crime, which became a decisive factor in 2006; struggles among different social groups, for example, campesinos engaged in land disputes; and finally, political violence committed by police officers, the armed forces, militants of the country's political parties and guerrillas or insurgents.

A reading of this document shows that Guerrero is a society based around the exercise of violence instead of respect for the law, around the premodern practice of taking justice into one's own hands and around the predominance of caciques and private security forces, a place where authoritarianism and macho behavior impose themselves on individual and collective coexistence, both public and private. As a means of self-defense, some parts of Guerrero have seen the emergence of "community police," as in other parts of the country.[44]

The harsh effects of poverty, inequality, marginalization.

The "Mexican Moment" that the government announced in 2014 sounds like a cruel joke.

Guerrero has been reluctant to accept the modern transformations of coexistence, which has made it fertile ground for the arrival of organized crime and the development of criminal organizations. Community self-defense groups, which claim to fight criminals and assume responsibility for public safety, operate in 46 of Guerrero's 81 municipalities, affecting 65.47% of the state's population—and feeding the growing violence, which tends to normalize itself.[45] As expressed by a popular verse from the Costa Chica of Guerrero and Oaxaca:

> *En las ramas de un mastuerzo*
> *vino el aire y me torció;*
> *hay días que me tuerzo, tuerzo,*
> *hay días que ya me torcí;*
> *ora para destorcerme,*
> *sólo torciéndote a ti.*

> (Through the watercress
> The wind came and twisted me;
> There are days when I twist, I twist,
> Days when I've been twisted;
> Now to untwist myself
> I'll simply twist you around.)[46]

An operative intelligence analyst who works for government agencies taught me that detecting, collecting and ordering informational material imposes a model of understanding on the event, issue, problem, process or episode being investigated. For those who know how to read their underlying meaning, collecting and classifying data soon reveals lines of convergence or divergence among the factors or agents present in a given situation.

In general, the prevalent position in the field of investigative journalism consists of adopting a restricted focus when trying to understand an issue or problem. A bad imitation, in other words, of the model of specialized academic research, centered around a given axis: the official document. Reporters therefore lack a broader perspective on the strategically determining factors of what they're investigating.

Strategy: a method or formula chosen to reach a desired future. Reaching an objective, for example, or solving a problem. Or turning planning and classification methods into an art and science, making them more efficient and effective. Today, governments and transnational corporations dominate the different planetary strategies of geopolitics and geostrategy.

Reporters, however, are required to avoid associations and speculations on the effects of geostrategy on domestic and international politics, even when a large part of intelligence analysis, whether operative or prospective, depends on establishing convergences, conjectures, calculations and well-founded speculations that tend to make use of patterns, interpretation schemes, analytical proclivities.

When faced with investigations into government affairs, reporters are induced to center themselves on the official story or to use it as a basis, becoming mere signal boosters and regular clients of the source that they should be systematically questioning through alternate points of view.

When I began to investigate the murders of women along the U.S./Mexico border, the first thing I observed was the informational disaster on the part of the Mexican authorities, who wanted to hide the obvious: a series of specific crimes committed with a recurrent *modus operandi* and victimology, as detected by external criminologists. What would later be termed femicide originated in specific criminal cases in which local police officers, government officials and businessmen were complicit with organized crime.

These crimes were "solved" by blaming innocent people using false testimonies, confessions obtained through torture and other, similar machinations. Dozens of these crimes remain unpunished and the victims and their families are still waiting for justice to be done.

That line of corruption built a pyramid of interests of such unprecedented breadth and scope that the government is still covering it up at the municipal, state and federal levels. Economic and political powers, allied with criminal power, created a network of shared interests whose impact would endure in Mexico's public life. The word "corruption" is insufficient for the magnitude of this evil.

Many investigators, including myself, were able to document the events along the border as they occurred. And we did it by analyzing the facts and evidence to see if they were consistent, if information was missing or if we should discard disproven theories, as well as by underlining the relevant historical, sociopolitical or anthropological context. The facts were proven to be true and they were differentiated from any narrative complement in the text. When framed in such a way, who could fail to understand? No one, except for those who refused to read the words in front of them, instead assuming things outside the text.

My professor in operational intelligence analysis insists that the logic of analytical arguments has to be explained and their flaws exposed, prioritizing relevant factors, uncovering hidden connections, differentiating reiterations, expanding informational inputs and predicting future developments.

I have learned that investigation is a job where one needs to trust in one's self as well as in the human factor (one informant leads to another, who then leads to clues, evidence and new puzzles). A strategic horizon is needed in order to determine the proper scale. Once a matter has been taken up, it needs to be pursued with a strong basis in fact above all other considerations, because if it's something that determines or concerns the collective, it's possible that the underlying mechanism can reappear elsewhere.

The rest is patience, time, a place to meditate. I will venture a definition that has been useful, at least for me, in guiding my work: investigating events is an art of rationality, logic, criticism, intuition, practicality, experimentation and openness which tends to be expressed in writing.

The barbarism in Iguala had been brewing for some time before the night of the 43. The municipality of Iguala, where these events occurred, had a homicide rate per 100,000 residents that was 210% higher than the national average in 2013.[47] In this process of disintegration, where was the government, where was the state?

In previous years, the criminal organization Guerreros Unidos, with the complicity of Iguala Mayor José Luis Abarca and the collaboration of the municipal police (whose commanders were ex-military), generalized the practice of extorting the citizenry.

Iguala became a strategic point for producing and trafficking heroin, as well as for transporting cocaine from South America. And while Guerreros Unidos may dominate the municipality, their control of the territory is disputed by Los Rojos and La Familia Michoacana.

Abarca, arrested for his alleged participation in the massacre of the Ayotzinapa 43, had been part of the leadership of Guerreros Unidos even before he became mayor. Abarca's wealth and political connections grew to such an extent in such a short time that he opened a four-hectare shopping mall known as Galería Tamarindos in 2008, home to major corporations such as McDonald's, Cinepolis, Mega Comercial Mexicana, Coppel, etc. Part of the land on which the mall was built had been donated by the Defense Secretariat.[48]

In 2013, Abarca was accused of assassinating three local activists and a government employee. The network of complicity at the local level went up to the state government of Guerrero and beyond: his political connections and sympathizers included members of the PRD and other leftist organizations, such as the National Regeneration Movement (MORENA) and its leader, Andrés Manuel López Obrador, who was aware of Abarca's dark past.[49] Following the tragedy, both parties hurried to distance themselves from Abarca even though they had previously supported him.

Abarca's wife, María de los Ángeles Pineda, also maintained connections with this criminal organization, both directly as well as through her mother, her two brothers and an in-law. After arresting the couple, the federal government announced that Guerreros Unidos regularly received two to three million pesos (between 100,000 and 200,000 dollars) from the mayor—monthly, bimonthly, weekly—of which at least half went towards buying off the local police force, in which the criminal organization also had say over the hiring of officers.

This *modus operandi* allowed local authorities to directly employ criminals as government agents, allowing them to openly carry out illegal operations: police-sicarios. The alegal structure of the Mexican state (outside the law and violating the law while pretending to respect it) thus produced its most savage incarnation.

The government's own account strengthens my convictions regarding the serious omissions and oversights in this case. The official narrative is inconsistent: the crimes committed in Iguala are a local matter, exceptional and limited in scope. The criminals are in jail awaiting trial, the federal government is not responsible and the Mexican state has nothing to do with these events.

The Mexican Constitution states that "the state must prevent, investigate, penalize and redress human rights violations." In light of these principles, how can we justify the lack of preventive measures in Iguala, how can we defend the negligence of the police, the armed forces and other government agencies at the time these barbarous acts were occurring? No formalism can excuse the government from respecting the spirit of constitutional principles.

In the United Mexican States, all individuals shall be entitled to the human rights granted by this Constitution and the international treaties signed by the Mexican State, as well as to the guarantees for the protection of these rights. Such human rights shall not be restricted or suspended...

The rise of the empire of crime forms part of our institutional disaster. I wrote in 2009 that the deluge of organized crime in Guerrero dates back to 2006, when the mutilated heads of two police officers were found on top of the exterior wall of a government building in central Acapulco. Two weeks beforehand, these police officers had participated in a shootout with drug traffickers in which two people died and close to 20 were wounded.[50]

Among the dead was a crime boss. Next to the heads, the sicarios taped a poster to the wall with a written warning: "So that you'll learn respect." The massacres had begun.

There used to be only two criminal organizations in Acapulco: the Juarez Cartel, whose malcontents would leave to form the Sinaloa/Pacific Cartel, and the Gulf Cartel. There was a public, countrywide struggle between these two organizations and their enforcers, who were respectively called Los Pelones or Chapos of Sinaloa and Los Zetas del Golfo, the latter deserters from elite units of the Mexican Army who would form a cartel of their own with the passage of time.

From then on, insecurity and violence took over the entire state of Guerrero, configuring a territory of low-intensity warfare and the normalized application of alegal power as these organizations experienced splits and others arrived. This territory also encompasses the state of Michoacán along with parts of Oaxaca, Morelos, Chiapas and other adjoining areas.

Recent information indicates that 10 criminal organizations currently operate in Guerrero, occupying or traversing at least 65 of the state's 81 municipalities. Before 2006, besides the Sinaloa/Pacific Cartel and the Gulf Cartel, the Oaxacan organization of Pedro Díaz Parada also had a presence in the state, albeit a less important one.[51]

When the Beltrán Leyva brothers broke with the Sinaloa/Pacific Cartel in 2008, they strengthened their presence in Guerrero by uniting with the Zetas. The result was increased violence and the fragmentation of the Beltrán Leyva organization into smaller groups that nevertheless had a strong local/regional impact: Guerreros Unidos, the Independent Cartel of Acapulco, La Barredora, Los Rojos, Cartel of the Sierra, Los Ardillos, Los Granados...

I remember when, halfway through the previous decade, a Mexican academic and politician privately confirmed the rumored anti-drug strategy that the United States had recommended for Mexico at the first summit of the Security and Prosperity Partnership of North America (SPP) in 2005 (later augmented by the Mérida Initiative in 2008). Those responsible for implementing this strategy told him directly, in a closed meeting, that internal struggles and betrayals within criminal organizations had to be induced through favoritism towards some and persecution of others so that they would exterminate each other.

With the passage of time, this formula and the experimental strategy of war as a means of "civilizing" an entire country has resulted in catastrophe.

In 2007, the criminal organization La Familia Michoacana expanded into Guerrero, establishing a presence in the Tierra Caliente and part of the Costa Grande. Thanks to its organizational capacity, resources and lethal power, as well as its experience in mobilizing people in an analogous territory, by 2008 La Familia Michoacana was able to dominate western Guerrero, as well as parts of the northern and central regions of the state, where it negotiated a mutual respect agreement with the Sinaloa/Pacific Cartel.

In their fight against these two cartels, the Beltrán Leyvas and their successor organizations entered local communities to establish control over common criminals and corrupt municipal authorities, promoting the growth of gangs under their control and ratcheting up kidnapping, extortion, human trafficking and other criminal industries.

When the Knights Templar split from La Familia Michoacana, they positioned themselves in the Tierra Caliente and in that part of the Costa Grande near the state line with Michoacán, which includes Ixtapa-Zihuatanejo. The regions of both states that border Mexico State also fell under their dominion.

To illustrate the power of organized crime in Mexico, it's enough to state that the Knights Templar control iron exports to China and La Familia Michoacana is involved in smuggling uranium, a key element from the geostrategic perspective that is mined from the Guerrero municipality of Arcelia.[52]

In 2012, the Jalisco New Generation Cartel (a revival of the Sinaloa/Pacific Cartel) entered Guerrero and all of the state's criminal organizations began to fight for supremacy, alternating in their temporal dominion over the state's municipalities, localities and transit routes.

Guerrero, like Michoacán, has strategic value due to its Pacific ports (Acapulco, Zihuatanejo, Lázaro Cárdenas), whose prime importance comes from their role as disembarkation points for large-scale shipments of drugs and other illicit substances, as well as focal points for drug sales, especially to domestic and international tourists.

Both states also contain important routes for transporting drugs to the country's center and north. While both Guerrero and Michoacán are territories engaged in low-intensity warfare, other high-risk factors still persist, such as ethnicity, violence, polarization and fragmentation around public issues where politics and the economy interact. The seeds of a war that can escalate in the future.[53]

In 2015, the government announced that the Knights Templar and La Familia Michoacana were in a state of collapse, while the Jalisco New Generation Cartel and Los Viagra were on the rise. The eternal return of the same, with only the names and faces of the criminals changed.

This leads me to the figures that the government has tried to cover up, both domestically and abroad: 33.1 million crimes were committed in Mexico in 2013; only 6.2% of these crimes were investigated. There were, in other words, 31 million unpunished crimes. In Guerrero, the impunity is absolute: nearly all crimes (97.6%) go unreported.[54]

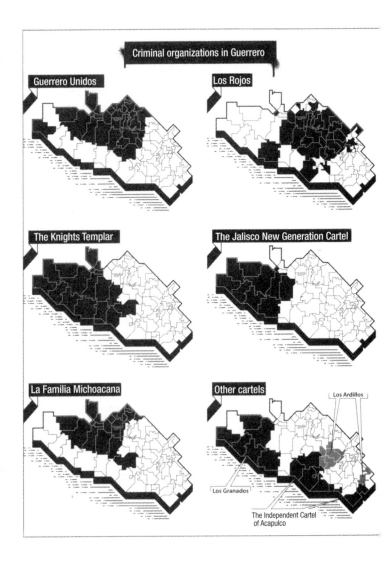

Criminal organizations in Guerrero

Guerrero Unidos

Los Rojos

The Knights Templar

The Jalisco New Generation Cartel

La Familia Michoacana

Other cartels

Los Ardillos

Los Granados

The Independent Cartel of Acapulco

In 2015, the government announced that crime was on the decrease in Mexico, but they forgot to include one decisive factor: crimes increasingly go unreported. And this affects the number of criminal investigations.[55] For the government, a crime that goes unreported does not exist. Evil imposes itself: the concrete evil of abuse and injustice.

Quieting this perverse emanation, trying to hide it, trying to relativize it with irrelevant comparisons or manipulated data, means a politics of barbarism from the institutions themselves.

In such circumstances, the anomalies, interests and benefits involved become strategic for all internal and external agents that form a part of the immediate context. Mexico's government and society find themselves facing a major challenge of uncertain duration.

My desk is covered with photographs, documents, official reports, court transcripts, witness statements, audio recordings and videos that testify to the extreme cruelty that disturbed one summer night in a city in southern Mexico and my head involuntarily rings with that song-psalm by Robert Plant: *Satan, your kingdom must come down / Satan, your kingdom must come down / I heard the voice of Jesus say, Satan, your kingdom must come down...* And I ask myself why the Anglo-American narrative relates the content of evil with individual acts committed by shadowy persons while making almost no reference to the political framework that makes them possible.

The perversion that I am examining implies so much more than mere crime or an ambition for supremacy on the part of certain individuals: it infests the conventional order of the world in which we live.

7

THE REAL COUNTRY AND
THE FICTIONAL COUNTRY

On the afternoon of September 23rd, 2014, three days before the acts of barbarism in Iguala, President Enrique Peña Nieto entered the Waldorf Astoria on New York's Park Avenue to receive the Appeal of Conscience Foundation's World Statesman Award.[56]

I once visited the hotel myself and I can picture the ceremony: candlelight falls on the furniture and potted plants that line the marble hallways, subtly perfumed by the dust and carpet freshener exuded by the red, white and gold rugs, offering a charming, grandiloquent warmth: the world of exclusive opulence.

Peña Nieto accepted his trophy, a metallic globe mounted on a pedestal, and listened to a speech by Henry Kissinger, who synthesized the arguments of his latest book, *World Order*, which had gone on sale just days beforehand. The former secretary of state advocated a world government led by the

United States and based around four pillars: ultra-liberal democracy, market economics, free trade and the rule of law.

The orator repeated his rejection of the sovereignty of the nation-state ("A core part of the problem is that the economic system has become global, while the political structure of the world remains based on the nation-state") and argued for imposing the "American perspective" on the planet. His words were sealed with applause.

In just two short years, Peña Nieto reached the height of international prestige for passing educational, telecommunications and energy reforms that had been delayed for decades. Both domestically and abroad, the achievements of his reformism were held up as an example for the world and there was much praise for the "Mexican Moment" and the charisma of the "Aztec Tiger" who was "saving Mexico." Many other, similar titles were bestowed upon him as he crystallized public policy under the guidance of large North American and international financial institutions.

These legislative reforms, achieved by signing a pact with the leaders of the country's main political parties so as to avoid an open deliberative process in the Senate and the Chamber of Deputies, became the subject of a government propaganda plan of planetary scope.

It's estimated that the Mexican government spent 600 million dollars on propaganda in just a year and a half.[57] The government's plan seemed to work until the reality of the country got in the way, in all of its profound contradictions: poverty, inequality, low economic growth, insecurity, violence, corruption.

I form part of the generation that witnessed the period of neoliberal reforms that began in the 1980s and came to a climax when the Mexican government signed the North American Free Trade Agreement (NAFTA) with the United States and Canada in 1994, an event that would lead to the establishment of an ultraliberal geopolitics of planetary scope.

At the time, it was said that this trade agreement would lift Mexicans out of poverty by creating new jobs in the manufacturing industry; the argument was that Mexico would "export goods, not people."[58] It was also argued that the country would become part of the first world. Since then, we have been facing one of the great problems of our time: the confusion between concrete politics and propaganda.

And so Mexico gained admission to the Organization for Economic Co-operation and Development (OECD), which brings together the world's most important industrial nations. Twenty years after the implementation of NAFTA, a large part of its promises remain unkept. Mexico's economic growth during this period was among the lowest in Latin America and its levels of poverty and inequality are the same as they were before NAFTA.

The numbers are clear: while the poverty rate has remained stagnant over the past two decades (around 52%), the country's population growth during this period means that there were 14.3 million more Mexicans living in poverty in 2012 than there were in 1994. Unemployment also increased and Mexico lost some 4.9 million jobs in the family farm sector due to the conditions of the post-NAFTA period, which included lower prices for staple foods and a reduction in government subsidies.

In those years, exports and foreign investment increased like never before, but NAFTA also produced a flow of people across the border: over 10 million Mexicans migrated to the United States. The post-Mexican condition is dominated by the effects of civil difficulties.

In my mind's eye, I can see the Museum of the City of Mexico, housed in the former palace of the Counts of Santiago de Calimaya, whose walls boast paintings of robust, dark-skinned men and women who show off their nudity in a colorful, patriotic atmosphere: the red, white and green of the Mexican flag and tones of earth, sand, ash, gold, ochre, volcanic rock evoking congealed blood and black basalt can be seen in huts and ruined dwellings in the desert or along the banks of dry riverbeds that are surrounded by children, also naked, their swollen bellies showing their malnutrition, sometimes in the midst of festivities featuring mariachis or traveling musicians with snowy volcanoes in the background. With laughter, beer, pulque, liquor, they celebrate the eternal festival of a lost Mexicanity that can only be redeemed by the echo of the past: pop culture icons from decades gone by; the Virgin of Guadalupe/Tonantzin reappearing in her domestic and portable aspect, intimate and telluric; withered boughs, the underworld that irrupts from intrahistory: tradition renewed again and again. The dream-nightmare that accompanies the times juxtaposed on the south and north of the Río Grande/Río Bravo.

These large-scale paintings by Daniel Lezama, which were collected years ago for the exhibition of his work at the Museum of the City of Mexico, come to mind again and again: they express the post-Mexican condition better than anything else. Pain, irony, laughter, fervor, the perplexity of a mestizo race with roots in both heaven and earth. Corporeal, urgent, overwhelming, exultant fictions that in the end are devoid of scandal, family portraits of a community and of the communities that add up to a country. Scenes constructed for quiet, illuminating contemplation. The Mexico that the modernizers have always tried to annihilate with their occasionally insipid, occasionally barbarous prescriptions.

Just before Peña Nieto received the World Statesman Award, his administration announced that violent crime was on the decline and that Mexican soldiers would participate in UN peace-keeping missions as part of the multinational forces known as the "blue helmets." Yet another example of the contradiction between desire and reality. A proclamation of world peace while the country is being torn apart by war.

While the world was celebrating the Aztec Tiger, the government and media of the United States were backing an international campaign against the Mexican Army over its human rights violations: 22 people were executed before dawn on June 30th, 2014 by soldiers engaged in law enforcement activities in Tlatlaya, Mexico State. The executions occurred in a warehouse guarded by armed men.

The army described the operation as a shootout in which 22 people died and one soldier was wounded. Shortly afterwards, however, the Associated Press revealed that the dead had been executed: not only could this be proven by analyzing the crime scene, but there was also a surviving witness.

At the beginning of September 2014, a Mexican magazine published an eyewitness account of the executions from a woman known as "Julia."[59] On September 19th, 2014, State Department spokesman Jeff Rathke told reporters that the U.S. government had been following the case from the beginning and that Congress was monitoring the implementation of the Mérida Initiative (the bilateral security cooperation agreement signed by Mexico and the United States in 2008, which supposedly ensures that human rights will be respected).

On September 25th, Mexico's Defense Secretariat (SEDENA) announced that eight soldiers had been arrested for their alleged responsibility for the crimes committed in Tlatlaya. One day later, 19 revealing images of the massacre were leaked to the press. The non-governmental organization Human Rights Watch (HRW) argued that they tore the official story apart.

The Mexican government said that the events in Tlatlaya were an exceptional case. It would soon be proven that not just the army involved in the cover-up but also the government of Mexico State, and that the executions were carried out under a Code Red combat protocol: if soldiers are attacked they must kill all of their assailants, taking no prisoners.[60]

International organizations such as the UN and Amnesty International have stated that human rights violations such as torture are not only regularly committed by Mexico's police and armed forces, but are also tolerated by the government: torture is widespread across the country.[61] The Mexican government has once again denied the seriousness of the problem.

The domestic and international scandal over the barbarism in Iguala and the 43 disappeared students provoked a worldwide clamor for justice for the victims and their families, which was fostered by social networks and emerging platforms: slogans such as "We Are All Ayotzinapa" and "Ayotzinapa: A Crime of State" were repeated during the hundreds of protests, rallies and solidarity actions held across the country and abroad.

Ever since the 1968 student movement, Mexico's students have incarnated promise and renewal. An attack on students, such as with the barbarism in Iguala, can unleash an exceptional pain and indignation. In a country where young people are the majority, as is the case in Mexico, killing students is more scandalous still.

As I have shown, young people face a present and future marked by violence, limited opportunities and the profound inertias of poverty, unemployment, precarious healthcare, educational and cultural erosion, etc. In 2014, the three leading causes of youth mortality were homicide, violent accidents and suicide.[62]

The way in which young people express their personal and collective malaise is by shouting their inconformity at protests, where some of them opt for vandalism and other acts of desperation while the authorities alternately remain indifferent, make threats using the mass media (radio, television, newspapers) or spread calumnies, admonitions and accusations that tend to criminalize those who question or reject the government's narrative.

As domestic protests grew and the international community began to distance itself from the Mexican government over the 43 disappeared students and the other murders committed by police-sicarios, the government tried to reduce the fallout by presenting these events as isolated incidents.

Playing down the importance of an event, and doing so in an impartial tone, is a common practice in the construction of an official narrative and is carried out by an array of spokespeople and spin doctors, experts in propaganda and the manipulation of information.

Norberto Bobbio has written that, in political discourse, it's common to turn to the legitimacy provided by lies, simulations and dissimulations, and that prudence is considered a higher virtue: "Prudence concerns speaking and remaining silent, not saying everything but instead revealing just one part of the truth, saying nothing, telling half-truths, reticence."[63] Propagandists also abuse euphemisms, those terms which substitute others that, out of prudery, convenience, opportunism or self-interest, cannot be pronounced. Or they exhaust themselves in rhetorical nuance, in the occultation that obsesses itself with avoiding or covering up the facts.

Speaking before the Inter-American Commission on Human Rights, a Mexican diplomat denied that his government has a policy of violating human rights. His prudent words overlooked the fact that crimes can be committed both by commission and omission, and that the Peña Nieto administration refused to act in such a way that would have prevented the rule of law from deteriorating to such a point in Guerrero that a municipal government could have committed such serious crimes.

And that the armed forces may have even participated in the barbarism in Iguala, just as they did in the Tlatlaya massacre or in the execution of 72 Central and South American migrants in San Fernando in 2010, to which we can now also add the extrajudicial executions of 16 civilians in Apatzingán in 2015.[64]

Although there's no explicit policy to violate human rights, these violations nevertheless exist and are tolerated by the political system. This is why so many are protesting against normalized barbarism. There are some who say that, instead of accusing the state, people should be protesting against criminals, but this is a self-interested absurdity: this argument aims to distract attention from the primordial problem, which is the responsibility of the state itself.

The arrest of former Iguala Mayor José Luis Abarca and his wife María de los Ángeles Pineda at the beginning of November 2014 formed the basis for the official Ayotzinapa investigation. The former was accused of being the intellectual author of the enforced disappearance and murder of the 43, as well as the 2013 assassination of an activist named Arturo Hernández Cardona and his two companions, Ángel Román Ramírez and Félix Rafael Balderas Román. The couple was also accused of running the criminal organization Guerreros Unidos together.

Days later, when the federal prosecutor announced the discovery of two bags filled with ashes and bone fragments in the Cocula garbage dump, located 22 kilometers from Iguala, the families of the victims refused to accept the official story.

What's so strange about all this is that, according to what we know, the situation was in the hands of the federal government from the start, as several witnesses have mentioned the presence of soldiers and state and federal police that bloody day. The discovery of the human remains was announced more than one month later. In intelligence circles, a video circulated showing alleged images of the massacre that night.

The distrust and rage directed at the authorities, which comes not just from the families of the victims but from society as a whole, is above all due to the fact that the Attorney General of Mexico (PGR) held on to so much information regarding the case that, weeks beforehand, the human rights activist Father Alejandro Solalinde was able to reveal information that would show up in the official investigation a month later.

On the pretext of gaining time to carry out the necessary inquiries, the federal government manipulated the investigation and waited to reveal the information it had on the case; at the same time, it fooled the families of the victims and the general public with a supposed search for the students "by land, air and sea," making use of aerial drones, when they already knew where they had allegedly been executed, as well as all the other details that would later be revealed by the prosecutor.

According to Solalinde, the arrest of Abarca and Pineda was staged in Iztapalapa (a zone of Mexico City with strong support for the leftist PRD), far from where they were actually arrested (perhaps the state of Veracruz), in order to emphasize their membership in the aforementioned opposition party and thus take political and electoral advantage of the situation.

For their part, the PRD and MORENA denied any political influence from the municipal government responsible for the barbarism of Ayotzinapa. The speculation with the pain of others, the management of an institutional crisis through a failed propaganda effort and the partisan accusations and denials all reflected the confusion of priorities and responsibilities.

President Peña Nieto didn't even dare to mention the disappearance of the 43 until 11 days after the incident, and it took him nearly a month to meet with the families of the victims: his opinion was that "the authorities in Guerrero" should "take responsibility themselves." Instead, he prepared for an official visit to China and encouraged the governor of Guerrero to resign, as occurred on October 25th, 2014.

In those days, it was also revealed that the First Lady's mansion, worth at least seven million dollars, was registered to the company that built it: a public works contractor with close ties to the federal government and prominent Chinese investors. China's economic penetration into Mexican territory, with the consent of the government, has displeased the United States.[65]

There were protests across the country and the entire world condemned the 2014 World

Statesman, who had failed on three key issues: human rights, governance and transparency.

The U.S. government has called the Iguala case "one of the most disgusting and repulsive crimes in the history of the human race." Yes: "in the history of the human race," even as it defends its bilateral collaboration with Mexico.[66] The United States has also distanced itself from the massacre of the 43, which it considers to be a Mexican affair, but where have its interests lain all these years, how have its intelligence and security agencies operated in Guerrero and how have they interacted with Mexico's politicians, soldiers and criminals?

I must say what nobody else wants to mention. Against silence, against hypocrisy, against lies, I must remember.

8

THE GAME BEHIND THE GAME

In the convergence of local and regional factors involving groups opposed to Guerrero's institutions, there are two determining geopolitical factors that are almost always minimized: the arms market and the drug market. And, above all, the ways in which they operate in the real world.

It's worth repeating that both of these factors converge in the dominion of the United States: the first in terms of the country's role as an arms supplier and in the supremacy of its armaments industry, which allows it to shape the fate of nations (as it sells arms to militaries and police forces as well as to criminals through the black market); the second in terms of its role as the world's largest consumer of drugs.[67]

In the backyard of the United States—that is, in Mexico and Central America—a strategic process is being implemented in which the United States and Canada (Mexico's NAFTA partners since 1994) are reassessing Mexican territory as a source of human resources (cheaper manual labor that is specialized for their mercantile or productive needs) and natural resources (mining, oil, natural gas, large-scale poppy farming and trafficking in other controlled substances).

This geostrategic phenomenon, which is tied to the security demands of the United States, is a taboo subject for most bureaucrats and the majority of analysts.

In 2007, for example, the Los Filos gold mine—the largest in Latin America—opened in Mezcala. It's expected to produce 60 million tons of gold over the next 20 years. Owned by a Canadian company and located 50 kilometers from Chilpancingo (as well as from the dissidents in Ayotzinapa), the mine has a gold belt that reaches the municipality of Arcelia and is also a source of silver, copper, zinc, iron and lead.[68] The plant has directly and indirectly created some 5,000 jobs; there are 3.5 million people living in Guerrero.

In 1993, Mexican law facilitated the privatization of the mining sector and promoted foreign investment by completely eliminating the royalty system, though it is common practice around the world. Mining companies now only pay the federal government 1.2% of the value of products exported and pay no state or local taxes. Between 2005 and 2010, for example, multinational mining interests operating in Mexico, led by Canada, made 552 billion pesos (36.8 billion dollars) but only paid 6 billion pesos in taxes (400 million dollars, around 1% of their revenue).[69]

In 2014, Guerrero produced over 60% of the country's supply of the opium poppy (*papaver somniferum*). According to the UN, the number of hectares of Mexican land devoted to this illegal crop have doubled since 2008. After Afghanistan, Mexico is the world's second-largest producer of opium. Opium poppies are primarily cultivated in Chihuahua, Sinaloa and Durango in the north and Guerrero in the south, where the opium harvest is concentrated in the municipalities of Iguala and Chilpancingo.[70] In this conjunction, we can see the problems of drug prohibition and the war machine, the geopolitical vector of the United States.

The origins of this conjunction must be examined, along with all of the other relevant facts that have been forgotten.

The large-scale cultivation of marijuana and poppies was introduced to the state of Guerrero by a CIA asset named Alberto Sicilia Falcón, of Cuban-American origin.[71]

This CIA asset was part of the "Mexican Connection" that took shape in Tijuana at the beginning of the 1970s under the protection of soldiers, government officials, police officers and even guerrillas that needed money and weapons. Its objective was to explore and exploit alternative territories to those in northern Mexico that had recently been subjected to the Mexican Army's Operation Condor and the complementary Plan Canador, short for cannabis and opium poppy (*adormidera* in Spanish).[72]

Since that time, the Mexican Army's 35th Military Zone, which is based in Chilpancingo, has had the formal responsibility to combat the cultivation of marijuana and opium, as well as those who exploit them.

As has been documented on both sides of the border, the United States government has two conflicting policies on drug trafficking: the first, which is formally stated, is to suppress and punish the production, distribution and consumption of controlled substances and is led by the Justice Department, the FBI and the DEA, among other agencies; the other is informal and confidential, consisting not only of political espionage and a variety of covert actions, but also the manipulation and control of criminal organizations and drug traffickers that are used to help the United States government achieve its geopolitical security objectives. These tasks are the responsibility of the CIA and other intelligence agencies.[73]

In the second case, we're dealing with the power exercised by the United States at the transnational level, which includes illegal arms trafficking, counterinsurgency and antiterrorism operations and the destabilization of foreign governments.

According to U.S. national security doctrine, covert operations must be planned and carried out in accordance with the government's military and foreign policies. The CIA is responsible for their execution. The national security strategy of the United States no longer recognizes the principle of state sovereignty, which dates back to the Peace of Westphalia in 1648.

Under the ideology of bilateral integration and cooperation between the United States and Mexico, recent years have seen the dismantling of the concept of sovereignty, which is one of the principles of the Mexican Constitution. In practice, the United States seeks the acquisition of Mexico's natural, energy and human resources as a means to safeguard its own geopolitical interests, as well as those of its corporations and citizens. In exchange, it offers the financing, advising and security needed for this appropriative process, which occurs with the consent of Mexico's political and economic elites.

Each day, the United States sells more and more weapons to Mexico (both legally and illegally) and has even secured Mexico's permission to carry out extremely risky arms trafficking operations, such as the so-called Fast and Furious affair (2006–2011) and its analogues, which emerged from an executive agreement between the governments of Mexico and the United States and were a total failure: the damage is irreparable.[74] The politicians who swore to obey and respect the Mexican Constitution ended up bowing to the United States national security doctrine.

At the beginning of 2015, the Mexican government proposed a reform to the Federal Law on Firearms and Explosives whose primary aim was to allow Immigration and Customs Enforcement (ICE) officers—as well as representatives of other U.S. government agencies, such as the CIA, the DEA, the FBI, the Pentagon, etc.—to bear arms in Mexican territory. The justification for this initiative was based on the need to generate "improved spaces of competitiveness" and "shared importance."

It has been known for some years now that armed agents of the U.S. government operate in Mexican territory. It's estimated that there are 25,000 of these agents carrying out covert operations in Mexico, with 55 bases around the country for their exclusive use. Between 2014 and 2015, the Peña Nieto administration purchased over 3.5 billion dollars in firearms and military equipment from the United States.[75]

The CIA station in Mexico has been strategic for U.S. covert operations in North America, Central America and the Caribbean, as has been proven in documents and testimonies on a variety of historical episodes from the overthrow of Guatemalan President Jacobo Árbenz (1954) to the assassinations of the journalist Manuel Buendía (1984) and the DEA Agent Enrique Camarena (1985), as well as the Iran-Contra or Irangate affair (1985–1986), in which the United States sold arms to the Iranian government and used the profits to finance subversive activities in Nicaragua, which included exchanging arms for drugs that were then sold in poor neighborhoods of Los Angeles, California, an operation that involved DEA and CIA agents.[76]

These CIA covert operations have their legal basis in mandates that are still on the books, such as the National Security Act of 1947 or National Security Council Directive No. 5412/2 (March 15th, 1954), which authorized military support for CIA black ops. The product of this synergy has been termed the Secret Team; one former special ops commander, Colonel L. Fletcher Prouty, described the Secret Team as security-cleared individuals in and out of government who receive secret intelligence data gathered by the CIA and the National Security Agency (NSA) and who react to this data, when it seems appropriate to them, with paramilitary plans and activities, as well as with training and "advising" to "friendly" or allied governments.

A flexible, mobile, intergovernmental and clandestine structure is used to carry out covert operations. Its function consists of trying to remain out of sight, often using stay-behind forces to ensure best results. A classic example of this is Operation Gladio in the 1970s, in which a secret CIA network under NATO command carried out an anticommunist campaign in Europe that included acts of terrorism.

The CIA, as has been documented by renowned historians of the agency, is no longer an espionage institution and has instead become a paramilitary organization dedicated to, among other operations, the selective assassination of its enemies.[77]

The framework or "architecture" that provides the legal basis for these activities is provided by a variety of executive orders issued over the years, such as Executive Order 12333 (Ronald Reagan, 1981), National Security Decision Directive 17 (NSDD-17, Ronald Reagan, November 23rd, 1984), Executive Order 13224 (George W. Bush, 2001), Executive Order 13355 (George W. Bush, 2004), the Military Order on the Detention Treatment, and Trial of Certain Non-Citizens in the War Against Terrorism (George W. Bush, November 13th, 2001) and the Memorandum of Notification on covert CIA activities (George W.

Bush, September 17th, 2001). Or the Patriot Act of October 26th, 2001, which expanded the powers of the United States government as part of the fight against terrorism.

In the United States Code, the CIA operates under the statutes of Title 50, which deals with war and national defense (often under direct presidential order); the Pentagon, in turn, must abide by the much more restrictive Title 10, which gives Congress the ability to impose limitations.

Robert Chesney has written that this architecture "serves to mediate the tension between the desire for flexibility, speed, and secrecy in pursuit of national defense and foreign policy aims, on one hand, and the desire to preserve a meaningful degree of democratic accountability and adherence to the rule of law, on the other. Of course, the legal architecture has never been perfect on this score."[78]

The CIA offices in Mexico are the largest in the Western Hemisphere outside the United States, both in size and importance.

According to U.S. government documents, Winston Scott, the CIA station chief in Mexico from 1956 to 1969, had 14 agents and paid collaborators within the Mexican government, including presidents Adolfo López Mateos (1958–1964), Gustavo Díaz Ordaz (1964–1970) and Luis Echeverría Álvarez (1970–1976), as well as other high-ranking functionaries, such as

Fernando Gutiérrez Barrios (who successively served as Federal Security Director, governor of Veracruz, Interior Secretary and senator).[79]

Scott gave Díaz Ordaz daily intelligence reports on the activities of revolutionary organizations in Mexico, which were then used by the government to carry out arrests and other acts of repression.

When we examine the public conduct and discretionality of recent presidents such as Carlos Salinas de Gortari (1988–1994), Ernesto Zedillo Ponce de León (1994–2000), Vicente Fox Quesada (2000–2006), Felipe Calderón Hinojosa (2006–2012) and Enrique Peña Nieto (2012–present), or that of government officials such as Eduardo Medina Mora or Genaro García Luna, it becomes clear that they have all been deferential or servile towards the requests of the United States at the cost of Mexican sovereignty.

One particular episode comes to mind that involves Winston Scott and his paid employee, Gustavo Díaz Ordaz. One day, the CIA station chief went to visit Díaz Ordaz in his offices. The president spoke so rapidly that the American could not quite understand him and said, in Spanish, "Stop, stop" ("*párese, párese*"), but the Mexican immediately got to his feet. "Why did you stand up?" asked Scott, intrigued. "Because you ordered me to," was the answer (in Spanish, the injunction *párese* also means "stand up"). Scott would laugh as he told the story.

Nobody capable of using logic can imagine that these practices and behaviors have completely disappeared in the attitude of the United States towards Mexico and its rulers. The hurry to surrender in order to remain on good terms with the representatives of the United States and its interests has destroyed Mexico.

Taken as a whole, this information—which is publicly available and self-evident from the point of view of strategic thinking, as I have labeled the understanding of geopolitical intelligence—tends to provoke a reaction of fear, an "I don't want to get into trouble," in other words, whose most frequent form is the banal practice of discrediting or overlooking information that alludes to these facts, when not directly misrepresenting them.

This attitude represents an extreme form of *negationism*: reality is denied in order to avoid a historic truth. It goes without saying: ignorance and government-sponsored stupidity are goods sold to the highest bidder. Disgracefully, such infamy abounds.

According to U.S. government documents, by 1978, the "Mexican Connection" operated by the CIA included not only producers and traffickers such as the Zambada family, but also a distribution network in the United States that extended throughout the

East Coast (New York, New Jersey) and the Western states (Las Vegas) and sold heroin and marijuana along with South American cocaine.[80]

The U.S. end of this connection was José Egozzi, an intelligence officer at the CIA and an associate of Sicilia Falcón who was linked to the agency's subversive operations in Portugal in 1974, as well as to the CIA's weapons shipments to Central America throughout the 1970s.

These documents tell us that DEA agents were aware that Sicilia Falcón not only had connections to the CIA station in Mexico City, but that the mention of his name would bring pressure from Washington, D.C. to drop the subject. U.S. federal agents have speculated that the CIA recruited him in Miami and promoted his rise, but that he "got too big for his britches" and had to be brought down.

Sicilia Falcón was arrested by the Mexican police in 1975. The DEA had been keeping a file on him for some time through its Central Tactical Unit 12 (CENTAC 12). Shortly thereafter, Sicilia Falcón broke out of Mexico City's Lecumberri Prison through a 40-meter tunnel in an escape that would become legendary. He was accompanied by his fellow prisoners Alberto Hernández Rubí, Luis Antonio Zuccoli and…José Egozzi.

It was not long before Sicilia Falcón was recaptured. He spent some time in Mexico City's

Reclusorio Sur and in 1991 he was transferred to the Almoloya de Juárez high security prison in Mexico State.[81] Among Mexican government officials, Sicilia Falcón could count on the protection of Miguel Nazar Haro, a police officer and CIA asset who would rise to become the director of the Federal Security Directorate (DFS).[82]

Beyond the mere destruction of crops, Operation Condor and Plan Canador reinforced the place of the subculture of illegal crops and commerce in northern Mexico and drove traffickers to take over other cities like Guadalajara (capital of the state of Jalisco), leading to the rise of the Guadalajara Cartel in the 1980s. The golden age of drugs in Mexico.

Besides displacing drug production to the south, these campaigns extended the fight against terrorism and subversion into Mexico's southwest, which was also the goal of the identically-named and U.S.-sponsored Operation Condor in South America. Extremes come to resemble each other.

The Mexican Army did its double duty of pretending to fight drug production (which managed to persist due to the corruption of soldiers, politicians and bureaucrats) while crushing Guerrero's guerrilla movements (which also survived). As the saying goes, bad weeds never die.

In 2015, the director of the CIA declared that world instability had returned to the levels of the

1960s, which implies a growth in ungoverned spaces, a spike in humanitarian crises and a surge in refugees, weapons and fighters across borders. He observed that, "By sharing intelligence, analysis, and know-how with these partner services, we open windows on regions and issues that might otherwise be closed to us. And when necessary, we set in concert to mitigate a common threat."[83]

These words are timely in a territory like Guerrero, where the geopolitical interests of different global powers (United States, China) coincide and where the old ties of the Latin American revolutionary left, now led by Venezuela, are still alive— just as there persist the risks represented by Islamic fundamentalism, organized crime and guerrillas such as the Revolutionary Armed Forces of Colombia—People's Army (FARC-EP), which allegedly has a presence in Guerrero.[84]

I have spoken with intelligence analysts and military affairs experts about the criminal-police operation against the 43 in Iguala that night.

Some of them describe it as an event characteristic of a new type of civil war dominated by avarice or material profit, which involves institutional corruption, organized crime and violence targeting competing groups, the civilian population and the police and armed forces. Those who share this opinion recognize the limitation of their interpretive model when asked about the historical weight of leftist revolutionary autarchy in Guerrero.

The situation in Guerrero in general and the episode in Iguala in particular seem to make more sense in the context of a local conflict between a variety of national and international political forces and interests where the anti-institutional struggle is dominant. The product is a low-intensity war, a brush war, a small war or an irregular war whose risks and threats will persist into the immediate and near future, above all from the perspective of the national security of the United States.

Taking this geopolitical perspective into account, one of these experts therefore recommended that I analyze the Iguala massacre as a confrontation that evokes insurgency and counter-insurgency dynamics. "You will discern a meaningful pattern," he added.

I have followed his recommendation.

According to U.S. military doctrine, in which Mexico acts as an ally under the protocol of the U.S. Northern Command, "Insurgency uses a mixture of subversion, sabotage, political, economic, psychological actions, and armed conflict to achieve its political aims. It is a protracted politico-military struggle designed to weaken the control and legitimacy of an established government."[85]

Counterinsurgency is a political struggle that incorporates a wide range of activities by the host nation's government, including security. And when the operational environment is not conducive to actions led by a civilian agency, "the joint force commander must be cognizant of and able to lead the unified action required for effective counterinsurgency."[86]

This military doctrine recognizes some prerequisites for insurgency: lack of government control, vulnerable populations, revolutionary leadership, opportunity, motives and means; all of these have been present in Guerrero for some time now. And it also points to the need for a specific preponderant *narrative*: the ability to shape the behavior of the insurgent ranks and the population at large, whose compliance and support are required due to the interdependence between the sociopolitical and military realms. In other words, what we have called the "revolutionary cosmovision" in Guerrero.

Under this doctrine, the involvement of the U.S. government in counterinsurgency operations "is based on three possible strategic settings: assisting an established host nation government, as an adjunct to U.S. major combat operations or U.S. operations in an ungoverned area."[87] Since 2005, when the SPP was signed, U.S. operations in Mexico have oscillated between these three settings.

Given this historic context, we must advance a hypothesis: the Iguala massacre bears a resemblance to the social cleansing operations carried out by soldiers and paramilitaries trained or supported by the U.S. government in El Mozote (El Salvador, 1981), Segovia (Colombia, 1988) and El Salado (Colombia, 2000).[88]

It's clear that, in the operational phase, the criminal-police action during the Iguala massacre was efficient, synchronized, coordinated and integrated,[89] as ordered by the Army Tactical Standard Operating Procedures, which Mexico's armed forces and police must recognize and follow under the framework of the U.S. Northern Command.

In its post-operational phase, it included not only crisis management and control of the criminal investigation but also adherence to the counter-insurgency narrative recommended by U.S. military doctrine, which consists of reinforcing the credibility and legitimacy of the government.[90]

A rather complicated operation for police officers and ordinary criminals under the command of an ignorant leader. Who could have assisted them? Perhaps soldiers trained in counterinsurgency tactics, the group of men in black clothes and ski masks that was seen that night. "It's obvious that they were highly trained," one witness has stated. Among the Iguala and Cocula police officers that have been arrested for the massacre of the 43, many have a military background: César Nava González (deputy director of the Cocula police, army signal corps), Darío Morales Sánchez (war materials specialist), Miguel Ángel Hernández Morales (military police) and Honorio Antúnez Osorio (war materials expert).

The practice of terror in Guerrero and Mexico as a whole (torture, enforced disappearance, extrajudicial executions, mass killings, cruel murders that involve mutilation or eye-gouging, the employment of criminals for specific tasks, etc.) replicates the counterinsurgency methods used in Vietnam under the Phoenix Program (1965–1972), which was designed and executed by the CIA and later replicated in Central America and Iraq. These social destabilization techniques, Douglas Valentine tells us, are now being applied in Mexico.[91]

This consummated pattern, which encompasses the military, paramilitary organizations and the political system, deserves an in-depth investigation. Why has the Mexican government kept its silence on this matter?

Since 2009, the Pentagon has trained over 9,000 Mexican soldiers in a variety of fields, at least 323 of them specializing in regional antiterrorism and insurgency and counterinsurgency tactics. A former commander of the 27th Battalion (Iguala)—a Special Forces soldier trained in intelligence and counterintelligence—used to accompany then-Mayor José Luis Abarca at public events. The army has been accused of disappearing half a dozen adolescents in 2010, when death squads made up of elite police officers were first detected in Iguala and rumors began to circulate of possible ties between soldiers and the criminal organization Guerreros Unidos. The National Defense Secretary would later admit that, among the 43, there was at least one active duty soldier who had infiltrated the group. It seems that the army was looking into connections between the students and guerrilla organizations.[92]

If we bring this historical context and background to light, then the deficiencies of the official investigation into the Iguala massacre and the true fate of the victims will become clear.

We can infer that federal prosecutors have imprisoned some of the criminals in order to cover for the rest (soldiers, marines and/ or paramilitaries). A matter that should be taken with the gravity it deserves: the authorities must carry out a comprehensive investigation into the actions of the army and navy in the Iguala massacre and their probable links with U.S. agencies.

According to intelligence sources within the Mexican government, the investigation into the disappearance of the 43 revealed the presence of CIA agents among the participants in the events in

Iguala. The FBI also intervened in the inquiry into the disappearances.[93]

Since the Mérida Initiative, undercover soldiers and agents of the CIA and DEA, among other U.S. government agencies, have been operating in Mexico and risk having their identities revealed, as occurred with the CIA agents Jess Hood Garner and Stan Dove Boss.[94] These two agents got involved in a shootout with Mexican federal agents "by mistake" while on their way to a secret U.S. base maintained by the Navy Secretariat in Xalatlaco, Mexico State, 180 kilometers from Iguala.

Both of these U.S. agents, like those operating in Iguala, disappeared without a trace and have since been under the protection of the United States government.

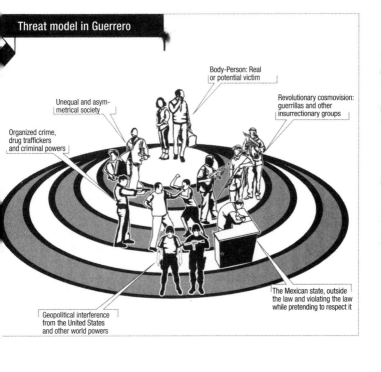

Threat model in Guerrero

Body-Person: Real or potential victim

Unequal and asymmetrical society

Revolutionary cosmovision: guerrillas and other insurrectionary groups

Organized crime, drug traffickers and criminal powers

The Mexican state, outside the law and violating the law while pretending to respect it

Geopolitical interference from the United States and other world powers

9

AT THE LIMIT

My cousin Lucila passed away in 2013, just days after my brother Pablo, who was the frontman of our blues-rock group Enigma! I have a photograph of the two of them together, taken when we were children; they are already perennial characters in the land of dreams and memories.

According to *Rolling Stone*, our self-titled album is among the 25 best Iberoamerican rock albums of the 1970s. Pablo was the protagonist of the story in those days, just as he was right up until his premature end. I remember him as a light in the darkness; his inexplicable death meant a cruel bifurcation in our shared path.

In the preceding decade, Lucila's son, a full-time professor, was disappeared in the state of Morelos: he had gone to the police to report a group of drug dealers in Cuernavaca that had been encouraging his students to start using. She looked everywhere for her son, reporting his disappearance to the authorities, speaking to the press, turning to human rights organizations, meeting with the governor, putting her trust in unscrupulous police officers who wanted nothing more than her money and hiring a clairvoyant, who only told her that her son was in a cold, dark place.

Lucila held on to the file on her son's disappearance and refused to give up hope: he would return one day. In the months before her death, my cousin called my sister. She sounded calm, unconcerned, resigned. My sister later described the call to me. Among other things, Lucila said that someone had approached her—she didn't say who—and told her to give up her useless optimism: her son had been killed the same day as his disappearance and his body had been disposed of. It would never be found.

Lucila died in peace. When my sister tried to call her to tell her about the death of Pablo, she was informed of Lucila's passing. The departed smile back at me from my photograph.

With the goal of avoiding the fall of his government, whose approval rating slipped from 46% to 39% in the final third of 2014,[95] President Peña Nieto announced a plan to strengthen the criminal justice system and the rule of law.[96]

This announcement coincided with the discovery of the bodies of 11 people who had been decapitated and partially incinerated in the Guerrero municipality of Chilapa de Álvarez.

In a solemn press conference at the National Palace, the president of Mexico unveiled his plan and stated, "We are all Ayotzinapa," words that only reinforced the skepticism and distrust with which his plan was greeted by the country's political parties, entrepreneurs, specialists and citizens.

The plan's 10 points did not include a single self-criticism or indictment of the political system's negative inertia; the explanation as to how the current crisis had come about would have to be found in previous administrations, while concrete progress would have to wait until an indefinite future. Nor were there any direct allusions to the reported corruption at the highest levels of his government.

In the meantime, the White House and the U.S. Senate increased their pressure on Mexico, while the powerful Council on Foreign Relations demanded a tougher line on the Peña Nieto administration and the foreign press criticized his hopeless plan.

At the beginning of 2015, the attorney general tried to quiet rumors that the 43 were still alive by announcing that there was "legal certainty" that the students had been executed by criminals affiliated with the Guerreros Unidos organization and that their bodies were then cremated, their ashes thrown into the Río San Juan. The perpetrators were convinced that the students had been "infiltrated" by the rival Los Rojos cartel, which allegedly maintains some sort of connection with the Revolutionary Army of the Insurgent People (ERPI).[97]

The attorney general declared that this was "the historic truth,"[98] a phrase that made it sound as if the case was closed. The negative reaction of the families was overwhelming and the prosecutor was forced to state that the investigation was still ongoing.

Two important episodes then occurred: the first was the appearance of the families of the 43 before the UN Committee on Enforced Disappearances, where they expressed their grievances against the Mexican government; the second was the government's "dialogue" with that same committee, in which they rejected the UN's jurisdiction in the Ayotzinapa case, even though Mexico is a signatory to the International Convention for the Protection of All Persons from Enforced Disappearance.

And so the game of legal-political strategies began: the families of the victims insisted on classifying the case as one of enforced disappearance, basing their arguments on testimonies regarding the direct and indirect participation of police officers and soldiers in the massacre (which had been recorded by the state prosecutor of Guerrero), while the attorney general spoke of crimes that fall under local jurisdiction (homicide, for example) and federal jurisdiction (organized crime, kidnapping), although he did state that he would insist on including charges of enforced disappearance.

To complicate things for the government, the Argentine Forensic Anthropology Team, which had been invited to Mexico to assist in the investigation, refuted the attorney general's explanations regarding the bonfire in which the bodies of the 43 students had allegedly been incinerated and brought to light many other irregularities, such as the broken chain of custody for much of the important physical evidence.

The response of the attorney general was brutal: he not only tried to discredit the team of forensic anthropologists for having questioned the government's "historic truth," but even impugned their professionalism. The Argentines were categorical: "Forcing the evidence to fit the testimony is not science."[99]

In the middle of this debate, it was announced on February 6th, 2015 that 61 bodies (the authorities would later say that there were only 60) had been found in an abandoned crematorium in Acapulco, Guerrero.

Immediately—without even waiting for the initial inquiries—the state and federal governments denied that organized crime was involved, stating that the crematorium was part of a plot to defraud the families of the deceased.[100] Bodies were embalmed but never cremated, with lime used to cover the smell of rotting flesh. The victims of this scam were given white sand instead of ashes.

A question arises: is it possible that criminals utilized this crematorium to make bodies disappear? The authorities have confirmed that this practice occurs in other states, such as Jalisco.

Through its Interdisciplinary Group of Independent Experts, the Inter-American Commission on Human Rights asked the Mexican government to classify the events in Iguala as a case of enforced disappearance; hence the desperation of the Mexican government, which promptly dismissed the prosecutor in charge of the initial inquiry. The International Criminal Court considers enforced disappearance to be a crime against humanity, which means that it has no statute of limitations. The group also recommended that the prosecutor open several new lines of investigation.

Six months after the massacre in Iguala, the judge assigned to the case threw out 50 charges against María de los Ángeles Pineda Villa, José Luis Abarca and over 50 police officers, alleged drug traffickers and individuals implicated in clandestine burials. A review of the initial inquiries and case files found them to be insufficient or poorly supported.[101]

Over the course of 2014, the authorities responded to the discovery of hundreds of clandestine graves in Guerrero by minimizing or avoiding the facts: they claimed that they were all isolated crimes. And they rejected the UN's recommendations on the matter.

The extermination of persons is self-evident in Guerrero and elsewhere. Why else would the prosecutor try to throw out the testimony of the student Luis Pérez Martínez? "The federal police showed up and fired on my classmates, wounding many of them and killing one," he said, though he was unable to identify the deceased. "Everyone got off the buses and some of us dropped to the ground. One of the federal police officers stood on the corner smoking a cigarette, gesturing for everyone to gather round, and then the officers started picking up shells so they wouldn't leave behind any evidence."[102] Attorney General Murillo Karam said that he was satisfied with the statement of the federal police director, who said that his men did not participate in the massacre in Iguala that night.

Following this logic, the Iguala massacre will soon disappear from official memory, like so many other cases in the past. In the hands of the prosecutor, the testimonies and even the events themselves will be annulled and erased. The word fades away and disappears in the irreverence of perverse authority.

To the contradictions, inconsistencies and lacunae of the official investigation into the massacre in Iguala, we can add the silencing of the witnesses. We're not even left with their murmurs and gasps for breath at the limit between life and death. They die a second time when their memory is erased.

In their desperation, the families of the 43 turned to a criminal, the boss of Los Rojos, who hung banners around Morelos in which he promised to tell them "the whole truth" of what happened to their children. "Please help us locate the whereabouts of our children," they begged him. "This bad government hasn't treated us seriously, on the contrary, they've hurt us with their lies. We are poor people and they have trampled on our dignity…"[103] In the meantime, the movement's more belligerent activists insisted on defying laws, regulations and constitutional principles, the government being unable to stop them.

In the process of formulating a medium-term political program, the families ratified a five-point plan at the First National People's Convention: that all 43 students arrested or disappeared in Iguala on September 26th and 27th be returned to them alive, that the material and intellectual authors of the crime be punished, that President Enrique Peña Nieto step down, that all political prisoners be released and that the Peña Nieto administration's structural reforms be overturned.[104] The 43: an enormous indignation, a strategy of endless confrontation with the state, its institutions and citizens unaffiliated with the cause.

My eyes half closed, the night of Iguala comes to mind. The movements of my eyelids trace an image of the events, which intertwine with deep vectors or infinitesimal, destructive lines: a rainy, impoverished city; irregular asphalt streets lined by walls sticky with the smell of fried food, gasoline and motor oil; the iron and steel of doorways and weapons; flesh violated by lethal bullets; shards of metal, glass and brick; students fleeing as their aggressors shout orders and insults; vehicles making abrupt movements; red and blue lights that intermittently capture the looks of fear on the faces of those furtively observing the desolation from their windows and hiding places. Some run, others trip and fall to their knees in the thick mud or pause in the face of imminent death. And in their mouths is the thirst of the irreversible as they are surrounded by a gray fog that absorbs their pleas and sobs, merging with the exhalations of decaying bodies unearthed from clandestine graves. Iguala: the name comes from the Nahautl word *yohualcehuatl*, which means "where the night settles down."

At the beginning of 2015, the immediate future looked adverse for Mexico's society and government due to the falling price of oil, the precarious peso, the economic weakness of the country's interior and the escalating social tensions. And due to the weight of the United States: its geopolitical interests, the use of its war machine on the pretext of wars on drug trafficking and terrorism, its incessant demand for drugs.

It's undeniable that both countries are historically responsible for the acts of barbarism committed in Guerrero against people they would rather cast off and forget.

Justice for the Ayotzinapa 43 and their families, as well as for all those disappeared and executed across the country, will persist in the memory of this generation as one of the greatest collective demands for transformation and genuine progress in Mexico and in its bilateral relationship with the United States.

The collective shame, the extreme impunity, the perverse vertigo is what I question.

The record is clear.

Tail of the lightning bolt, whirlwind of the dead. With the course they're on, their strength won't last long. Maybe they'll end up churned into foam or consumed by this wind of ashes. They might even get lost stumbling about in the dark. And when all is said and done, they are nothing but rubble.[105]

— Juan Rulfo

IN MEMORIAM OF THE 43[106]

1. Abel García Hernández
2. Abelardo Vázquez Peniten
3. Adán Abrajan de la Cruz
4. Antonio Santana Maestro
5. Benjamín Ascencio Bautista
6. Bernardo Flores Alcaraz
7. Carlos Iván Ramírez Villarreal
8. Carlos Lorenzo Hernández Muñoz
9. César Manuel González Hernández
10. Christian Alfonso Rodríguez Telumbre
11. Christian Tomás Colón Garnica
12. Cutberto Ortiz Ramos
13. Dorian González Parral
14. Emiliano Alen Gaspar de la Cruz
15. Everardo Rodríguez Bello
16. Felipe Arnulfo Rosas
17. Giovanni Galindes Guerrero
18. Israel Caballero Sánchez

19. Israel Jacinto Lugardo
20. Jesús Jovany Rodríguez Tlatempa
21. Jonás Trujillo González
22. Jorge Álvarez Nava
23. Jorge Aníbal Cruz Mendoza
24. Jorge Antonio Tizapa Legideño
25. Jorge Luis González Parral
26. José Ángel Campos Cantor
27. José Ángel Navarrete González
28. José Eduardo Bartolo Tlatempa
29. José Luis Luna Torres
30. Joshivani Guerrero de la Cruz
31. Julio César López Patolzin
32. Leonel Castro Abarca
33. Luis Ángel Abarca Carrillo
34. Luis Ángel Francisco Arzola
35. Magdaleno Rubén Lauro Villegas
36. Marcial Pablo Baranda
37. Marco Antonio Gómez Molina
38. Martín Getsemany Sánchez García
39. Mauricio Ortega Valerio
40. Miguel Ángel Hernández Martínez
41. Miguel Ángel Mendoza Zacarías
42. Saúl Bruno García
43. Alexander Mora Venancio (his ashes have been identified)

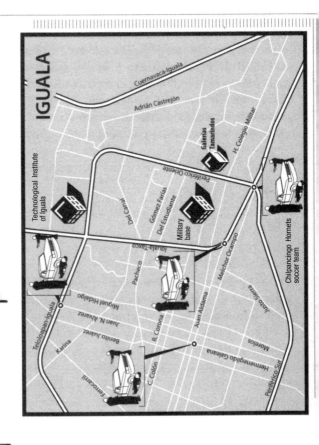

APPENDIX

THE OFFICIAL STORY

Ontiveros Alonso has postulated that, given the fact that: 1) there are Iguala and Cocula police officers who have said that they acted against the students on the direct orders of the then-mayor; 2) the police officers were ordered to turn the students over to members of the criminal organization Guerreros Unidos; 3) members of said criminal organization recognized the authority of the wife of the former mayor and affirmed that they were the ones who killed the students and burned their bodies; 4) the former mayor and his wife have been arrested and charged with homicide, kidnapping and organized crime, among other offenses, then from the perspective of penal dogma, the Iguala massacre could therefore be considered as a case of "intellectual authorship through control of the machinery of power," which should include charges of enforced disappearance.[107]

On November 7th, 2014, the prosecutor in charge of investigating the barbarism in Iguala, Attorney General Jesús Murillo Karam, called a press conference.[108] There he made the following announcement:

"It has now been 33 days since the state prosecutor of Guerrero turned over to us the case of the criminal acts committed on September 26th and 27th in Iguala, Guerrero. These have been 33 very difficult and painful days, above all for those who do not know the fate of their children, but also 33 days in which not a single day has gone by without an effort on the part of the federal government to locate the disappeared students.

"They have also been 33 days in which we Mexicans have felt distress and indignation over the disappearance of these 43 young students and we have all shown our support. The federal government has overseen a massive search effort that we can safely say has been one of the most complex operations in recent times. Ten thousand agents—including police officers, soldiers, sailors, prosecutors, investigators and other experts—have been searching the area for clues that will lead us to these young people.

"In a previous press conference, I mentioned that we have arrested those responsible for the deaths of six people in Iguala on September 26th, as well as those who kidnapped the rest and turned them over to the criminal organization Guerreros Unidos. Among them was Sidronio Casarrubias Salgado, the leader of the criminal organization that corrupted and took control of the municipal police forces of Iguala and Cocula. We also arrested those who had the authority and determination to order this painful event: the former mayor of Iguala and his wife.

"Today, several days after that press conference, we can announce further advances. We have arrested Patricio Reyes Landa, alias El Pato, and Jonathan Osorio Gómez, alias El Jona, who were located in the town of Apetlaca in Guerrero's Cuetzala del Progreso municipality. We were able to make these arrests because of the arrest of a third person by the name of Agustín García Reyes, alias El Chereje.

"These three men are members of the criminal organization Guerreros Unidos. Upon their arrest, they confessed to having executed a number of people who were handed over to them by the Iguala and Cocula municipal police. The federal government shares the belief held by the families of the victims and with society as a whole that this investigation must be transparent, which is why we have decided to report on our progress step by step, above all to the families who are suffering because of the disappearance of their children, but also to a society that has been aggrieved by a criminal act that cannot be tolerated and must not be repeated.

"Several hours ago, the families of the disappeared students heard the progress report that I'm now sharing with the rest of the country. I can understand the enormous pain that this information must cause the families, a pain that we all share. The testimonies that we have gathered, together with the rest of this investigation, unfortunately point to the murder of a large number of people in the Cocula area.

"In the search for the truth, my obligation is to be faithful to the investigation's findings, which is why I have called this press conference. We hope that the images and videos we are about to show you will allow citizens who have been victimized by the individuals shown to recognize them and report their whereabouts to the authorities. I want to be clear that we are giving a report on the investigation's progress, which should not be taken as its conclusion. The investigation continues. We will reveal our advances step by step.

"At the Isidro Burgos Rural Teachers' College in Ayotzinapa, a group of students boarded two buses owned by the Estrella de Oro bus line and headed towards the city of Iguala. When they reached the city's bus stations, they took possession of another two buses belonging to a different company. The former mayor of Iguala, whose police code name was A5, was the one who gave the order for the police to contain the individuals traveling in the four buses. This allegation is based on the testimony of David Hernández Cruz, the radio operator for the Iguala police force, and has been confirmed by one of the informants, known as "falcons," who received the message.

"As we have previously reported, this is when the Iguala municipal police took the lives of three of the students. At the time, the former mayor was at a ceremony in which his wife was reporting on her activities as director of the municipal Family Development Agency (DIF). An investigation is currently underway into María de los Ángeles Pineda and her possible involvement, alongside her husband, in money laundering operations. After the first clash with the students, who continued to advance through the city in their buses, the municipal police violently arrested them.

"With the support of the Cocula municipal police, they then took the group of students to a place known as Loma de Coyote, located between Iguala and Cocula. The investigation conducted by federal prosecutors has confirmed that this is where the municipal police turned the students over to the criminal organization Guerreros Unidos.

"The state prosecutor of Guerrero believed that the students were buried in a mass grave located in the Pueblo Viejo area. We have since been able to carry out a forensic analysis of the human remains found in the Pueblo Viejo mass grave and have confirmed that they are not those of the students. We have also been able to positively identify four of the people whose bodies were found in the mass grave and can confirm that they were murdered in the month of August—one month before the events in Iguala, in other words. The bodies of women were also found, while the group of students from Ayotzinapa was entirely composed of men. The facts that we have been able to confirm so far indicate that the Iguala municipal police were involved in the murder of the four individuals from the Pueblo Viejo mass grave whom we have been able to identify so far.

"At this time, Sidronio Casarrubias Salgado, the confessed leader of the criminal organization, was contacted by his second-in-command Gildardo López Astudillo, known as El Gil, who informed him via a cellphone message of the events that were occurring in Iguala, attributing them to a rival criminal group.

"Casarrubias Salgado was the one who signed off on the actions taken to 'defend their territory.' I'd like to ask everyone to closely examine this photograph of Gildardo López Astudillo, known as El Gil. This is the first time this photograph has been made available and it is of the utmost importance for the public to collaborate with federal prosecutors in locating this individual.

"The most recent arrests we have made, which include the three aforementioned material authors of the crime, have allowed us to understand the final link in this criminal chain. They declared that the municipal police turned a group of people over to them along the road to Loma de Coyote. They were unable to specify the exact number of people, but one of the arrestees estimates there to have been more than 40."

The prosecutor then referred to the declarations of Witness No. 1 (Agustín "El Chereje" García Reyes), who confirmed the presence and subsequent execution of the 43, adding:

"As we can see on this map, instead of taking the road to Pueblo Viejo, the place indicated by the Guerrero state prosecutor, the arrestees said that they took the highway to Cocula, heading to the garbage dump.

"They also said that they transported the students in two vehicles, one with a maximum load capacity of 3.5 tons and another with a lower load capacity. They drove these vehicles to the aforementioned garbage dump, which is located in a ravine and hidden from public view by a gate that restricts the public's access to the site.

"Here we can see images of the trucks that were used in the Cocula garbage dump. One of the criminals, who was designated as an informant (or "falcon") has declared that he saw these trucks pass through the location he had been ordered to watch. Two of the arrestees have declared that some of the people who were taken to the garbage dump were dead on arrival and that others were interrogated by members of the criminal organization in order to determine their identities and reasons for coming to Iguala. After these images, we'll look at copies of their confessions."

Before going on, the prosecutor then summarized the statements of Witnesses No. 1 and 2 (unidentified), who confirmed that the victims were students and that some of them were already dead (strangled) upon arrival at the Cocula garbage dump.

"The arrestees have declared that they then killed the survivors and took the bodies to the lowest part of the ravine, where they incinerated them. They kept watch over the fire for hours, working in shifts and adding diesel, gasoline, tires, firewood, plastic and other fuel that they found nearby. According to their confessions, the fire lasted from midnight until approximately 2 p.m. the following day.

"According to statements made by two of the arrestees, the fire burned until 3 p.m. on September 27th, but the heat made it impossible to manipulate the human remains until around

5:30 p.m. When forensic experts analyzed this location, they found ashes and bone fragments that correspond to human remains. Here are the images."

After showing images of the burn site to the reporters, the prosecutor summarized the confession of Witness No. 3 (unidentified), who described how the survivors were walked to the place where they were to be killed with their heads down and their hands on the back of their necks. Before being shot, they were then interrogated about their membership in a rival criminal organization, which they denied.

The prosecutor also stated that around 15 of the victims had already been strangled to death and arrived at the garbage dump in body bags. In one video, Witness No. 1 described how they disposed of the corpses. The prosecutor then resumed his speech:

"These statements have been corroborated by the declarations of two employees of the Cocula Department of Public Services, who later told the police that they were driving the garbage truck identified as Unit 01 when they were stopped by two of the men currently in police custody, who ordered them to turn back. This incident was first recounted by one of the arrestees and later confirmed by the municipal employees themselves, who recognized the arrestees as the individuals who had stopped them. The municipal employees have stated that they did not come forward out of fear of reprisals; given what they saw, this fear is understandable."

"Returning to our reconstruction of these events, the arrestees declared that, when the burnt bodies had cooled down, they received orders from a man known as El Terco to break up the charred bones and place them in black trash bags. According to their statements, all of these bags were emptied into the Río San Juan except for two, which one of the arrestees said he threw into the river without emptying out their contents."

To complement this account, the prosecutor showed seven videos in which those allegedly responsible for the massacre explained how they burned and disposed of the bodies. After the videos ended, the prosecutor began to speak again:

"Federal forces, investigators and forensic experts have examined the zone indicated by the arrestees (as you have been able to see in the images shown today) and carried out an exhaustive search of the Río San Juan. Tragically for our government institutions, a federal police agent drowned in the course of this search. Navy divers and a group of Mexican and Argentine forensic experts found the bags and what was left of their contents; one of them had remained closed and contained bone fragments, which we can confirm as corresponding to human remains." (Images of the human remains were then shown on the screen.)

"I'd like to ask you to keep looking at these images." (More photographs are shown.) "According to one of the forensic experts, the high level of degradation caused by the fire has made it difficult to extract DNA from these human remains, but we will spare no cost and will not give up on identifying the bodies until we have exhausted all of the scientific and technical options available to us.

"The federal government's forensic scientists and their Argentine counterparts are working hard to make a positive identification. To make progress towards the eventual identification of these human remains, the forensic teams have recommended that studies be carried out in the world's most specialized laboratories.

"After a series of phone calls and videoconferences with different laboratories, it was decided to carry out mitochondrial DNA studies. The team of experts agreed that the best place to carry out these studies is Austria's University of Innsbruck. When these international experts were asked how long these studies would take, they told us that, due to the complications presented by the extreme calcination of the remains, they can't give us an exact date.

"During this investigation, federal authorities have seized many weapons that formed part of the criminal organization's arsenal, including 50-millimeter firearms and 53,000 cartridges. This shows that the criminals we're up against are extremely dangerous. I want to make it clear that, from what we have seen so far in this investigation, there is no evidence that the Ayotzinapa students either supported or formed part of a criminal organization.

"Federal authorities are continuing to track down and arrest all of the criminals and their accomplices. We have arrested 74 individuals and there are warrants for the arrest of another 10. But we will arrest all those implicated." (Images of the arrestees are shown on screen.) "I must repeat that this investigation will remain ongoing until we have exhausted every possibility to identify the human remains found in the ravine and in the plastic bags recovered from the Río San Juan.

"In the meantime, for the purposes of this investigation, we will consider the Ayotzinapa students to be missing. As we have repeatedly stated, the investigation will remain open to scrutiny from the experts named by the families of the disappeared, as it has up until now.

"On the orders of the president, federal forces are actively carrying out one of the most extensive criminal investigations in recent memory. This investigation stands out for its use of technology and intelligence, as well as the coordination and distribution of tasks between different federal agencies. Making these images public is an obligation to society, a society that has been truly, truly offended, but making them public is also a call for us to find a way to ensure, as I have said before, that this never happens again. I'm at your orders."

This judicial narrative of the events in Iguala only multiplied the questions of domestic and international reporters, who tried to clarify the inconsistencies, contradictions and lacunae of Murillo Karam's words and images. The long round of questions and answers came to a climax when the prosecutor said, "I've had enough." And with that the press conference came to an end.

This phrase ended up exasperating the public. Three days later, the prosecutor found himself forced to explain it and put it in context, to little avail.[109]

The families of the victims and those who supported their cause completely rejected this version of events, especially the explanation as to how the bodies of the students were incinerated outside on a rainy day in which nobody saw a bonfire at the place in question: some experts have stated that incinerating the corpses was impossible under the conditions described by the authorities. A crematorium would have been required.[110]

Others responded that it was possible, at least in theory. The families of the victims embraced the historic slogan of the South American left as the basis of their sociopolitical strategy: "They were taken alive, we want them back alive!" They directly denounced the state, the armed forces and the police. And they insisted on continuing the search for the victims, including on military bases.

Counterpoint: In those same days, the commander of the 35th Military Zone in Chilpancingo—directly responsible for the troops of the 27th Infantry Battalion, accused by the students of threatening and intimidating them on the night of the massacre—was promoted to divisional general.[111]

The government's narrative on the 43, including the arrests and all corresponding legal explanations, is of an evident fragility as it has largely been based on confessions that the accused have refused to ratify on the argument that they were made under torture.[112] This all points to the absence of the rule of law in Mexico, above all with regard to the crimes committed on September 26th in Iguala, Guerrero.

In a society like Mexico (ravaged by economic crisis, insecurity and violence and weary of demagogy, lies and government ineptitude), the reactions of doubt and suspicion towards the increasingly discredited official narrative reflect a profound rupture between government and society and indicate the weakness of the nation-state's foundations, both at the present time as well as in terms of its future prospects.

Among the irregularities detected in the search for the victims, there's the fact that the search was only conducted in restricted areas, as the families have testified; more and better quality photographs of the Cocula garbage dump are also needed. The map of the grave sites and the *modus operandi* of the criminals should also be analyzed in greater depth, while technology should be used to locate more grave sites and independent experts should assist the government in its institutional duties. The lack of a proper reconstruction of events breaks with methodological protocols.

In terms of the official investigation, there's a prominent lack of hypotheses and lines of investigation, as well as at least one case in which the chain of custody for the physical evidence was broken by prosecutors. Much of the government's case rests on self-incriminating statements that were allegedly made under torture and much of the forensic analyses remain incomplete.

Likewise, there has been an unnecessary dispersion of the judicial process (thirteen criminal cases in six different jurisdictions), which limits its effectiveness, as well as the arbitrary elimination of testimonies that contained pertinent information; perpetrators were invented and these were the lines of investigation followed; there was negligence and delay in collecting evidence and identifying the alleged perpetrators, the families of the victims were caused unnecessary pain and there was a lack of clarification regarding cases of enforced disappearance in Guerrero—the convergent impunity, in other words. In general, there has been carelessness instead of comprehensive policy addressing enforced disappearances.

And, above all, we are faced with the refusal of the Mexican government to allow the soldiers of the 27th Infantry Battalion to be interrogated by international experts.[113]

In order to reverse the erosion of Mexico's institutions, which threatens social, community, family and individual life on a daily basis, we must:

1. Remove the Army and Navy from law enforcement duties while strengthening and overhauling the police.
2. Control the illegal flow of weapons into the country and implement a strategic program to dismantle criminal organizations.
3. Establish a development plan for towns, regions and states with high levels of violence in order to reduce poverty, inequality, violence and crime and to ensure the proper delivery of public services in terms of health, employment, housing, transportation, education, etc.
4. Make more productive investments in place of government spending on weapons and criminal policies based around state terrorism.

Violence increased in Mexico in 2016, particularly in the state of Guerrero. The government was forced to recognize that at least 50 criminal groups were operating in the state. And the kidnappings, executions and disappearances continued, as did the discovery of bodies in clandestine graves. Mexico's armed forces and police perpetuated their routine violations of human rights and the normalized practice of torture persisted despite the outcries and demands of the United Nations and other international organizations. The government was likewise unable to protect journalists from intimidation, censorship and violence: eleven reporters were murdered between January and July 2016.

The Interdisciplinary Group of Independent Experts issued two detailed reports (one in September 2015 and the other in April 2016) that rejected a large part of the official investigation into the disappeared students. These criticisms caused the government to launch a campaign, carried out through friendly news agencies, to discredit these international experts, including the Inter-American Commission on Human Rights and the Argentine Forensic Anthropology Team, while playing down their recommendations.

The pressure of the victims' families forced the government to accept a mechanism to follow up on the lines of investigation proposed by the

Inter-American Commission on Human Rights in the case of the 43 Ayotzinapa students.

And though seventy percent of Mexican citizens disapproved of the Peña Nieto administration and the spread of social unrest could be seen in the protests of leftist teachers and business leaders— the burden of poverty and economic crisis—the government exonerated those soldiers who had been accused of violating human rights in the Tlatlaya case, while federal judges rejected charges of enforced disappearance for the Ayotzinapa students: it would then be possible to uphold the "historic truth" or official story of what happened to the 43, despite all its deficiencies.

Meanwhile, the Mexican government undertook a series of measure to recover its lost credibility on several political and legal fronts, whether through the falsification of the country's true poverty rate, the proclamation of an alleged drop in crime or an assortment of legal-administrative palliatives for the problem of corruption.

On the pretext of utilizing alternate experts, the National Human Rights Commission sought to uphold pro-governmental positions: it affirmed that the bonfire in the Cocula garbage dump was possible and exhumed the the remains of Julio César Mondragón for a second autopsy, carried out more than a year after his murder and burial, which it used to conclude that the skin hadn't been peeled from his face by humans but had instead been eaten by some scavenging animal.

According to records provided by the telephone company, Mondragón's cellphone—which disappeared at the time of his death—was later used to make several calls from Military Camp No. 1 and the Center for Research and National Security (CISEN), both located in Mexico City.

Finally, the Mexican government repeatedly refused to allow the soldiers implicated in the events in Iguala that night to be interviewed in person by international experts as this would "put the legality of the investigation in jeopardy."

Neither the army nor the navy nor the federal police nor Mexico's intelligence agencies—never mind their U.S. counterparts—were investigated to discover the true fate of the disappeared students.

For them, their families, their friends and those demanding that justice be done, barbarism and amnesia must be punished. And it's imperative that we deconstruct the ontology of war and violence as an evolutionary or historical motor.

The absolute impunity of crime in Mexico has contributed to the creation of egotistical individuals who, ignorant of transcendental values, lack a sense of limits and are prone to violence or the use of force in settling social conflicts. Society has radicalized and there has been a rise in the lynching of alleged criminals and the theft of weapons from police officers, as well as their legal purchase by citizens. In sum, distrust of law, order, politics.

Faced with this situation, the United States government has shown that its two biggest priorities are the economy (trade, border customs, educational exchanges) and national security (the fight against terrorism and organized crime). In response, Peña Nieto reaffirmed his "absolute will to cooperate" with the president of the United States, whether they be Democrat or Republican.

Just days after Peña Nieto's inauguration, the protocol of the U.S. Special Operations Command, North (SOCNORTH), an adjunct of the United States Northern Command (USNORTHCOM) was activated in Mexico. Its purpose is to train Mexican soldiers, intelligence agents and police officers in counter-insurgency tactics in the fight against terrorism and drug trafficking. The Mexican government has sought to keep this secret.

At this geopolitical juncture, a disparity can be seen between the general objectives of the SPP-Mérida Initiative and its lethal effects on Mexico in terms of insecurity, instability and the infringement of human rights.

In the fall of 2016, the families of the victims have continued to demand that the authorities prosecute one Tomás Zerón, the official who invented the "historic truth," for violations of due process. He was instead rewarded by being appointed the National Public Security Council's Technical Secretary after he left the PGR (even though the agency's Department of Internal Affairs had itself noted the "irregularities" committed during his investigation). They have also denounced that the Mexican government has offered to give them money if they withdraw their claims.

The families have demanded that the PGR explain why one key fact was omitted from its investigation: the alleged culprit Sidronio Casarrubias Salgado (head of the criminal organization Guerreros Unidos) had a notebook that listed the commander of the federal police in Guerrero, Omar Hamid García Harfuch, as a "contact." García Harfuch would later take Zerón's place as Director-in-Chief of the PGR's Criminal Investigation Agency (AIC). What is hidden behind this network of complicity? Incidentally, a judge has ordered the release of Casarrubias Salgado, who had been charged with organized crime in connection with the kidnapping of the 43 students.

Against silence, against hypocrisy, against lies, we must insist on our conviction that the influence of the perverse has devoured civilization, the institutional order, the common good. And, above all, we must search for the truth.

Where are they?

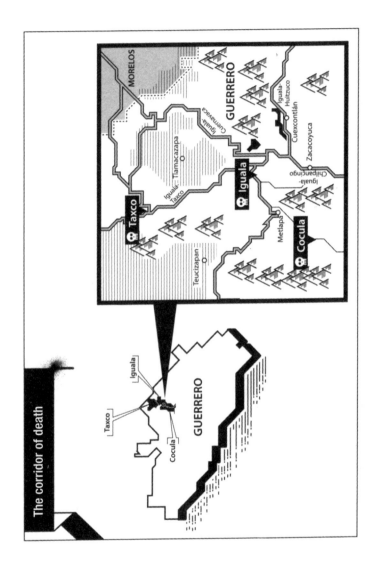

The corridor of death

PERSONAL EPILOGUE

The incineration of the 43 Ayotzinapa students is one of the most abominable images imaginable. But the idea of erasing all traces of one's victims by burning them has anthropological and criminological precedents in Mexico. And given the country's prevailing impunity, everyone is either the real or potential victim of an abuse, an injustice.

As is well known, the Vikings, Greeks and Romans used funeral pyres for centuries. It was believed that fire had powers of purification that could overcome the power of evil. Fire is still used in funerary rituals in India, while the Catholic Church has allowed for cremation since Vatican II. Death in a bonfire was reserved for heretics and witches. Death by fire symbolizes the greatest punishment: not only is it crueler for the victim, but it also represents a desire to reduce their body to ashes. The person as such is erased from the face of the earth and takes on the status of a mineral, with neither name nor memory. There is a case I would like to use to illustrate this.

If I evoke the name of a woman I knew some years ago (she was called Gloria), the image of her refined smile immediately comes to mind. A short, slender brunette, her features were as sharp as her charms. She worked in public relations in the entertainment world. With her exquisite blouses and plaid skirts, she was always the most radiant person at industry functions and press conferences. She was always the first to arrive and the last to leave.

Outside her professional life she was a mystery, at least to someone like me who didn't know her well. We exchanged civilities, greetings, gossip, jokes. One afternoon she introduced me to her younger sister, who had come to work at the office we shared. I can recall our laughter on those lazy afternoons of little work but much useless flirting. The business collapsed soon afterwards. And I stopped seeing Gloria and her sister.

I ran into Gloria at a party three or four years later. In those days, there was a scandal over the arrest of a group of drug traffickers who also practiced Santeria. It was a very unusual incident: a practitioner of Palo Mayombe who had attracted a court of sycophants, including one so-called priestess, and made a living by counseling singers and famous artists. This story was largely a lie; it would later be learned that it had been fabricated by the police in order to cover up their practice of extorting criminals.

Gloria avoided me that night; she knew that I had become a published writer. She was right to do so: I was dying to ask her what she knew about the shady dealings between that gang and a friend of hers, a singer and actress whose media relations she had been handling for some time.

I devoured the hours in trivial conversations with other partygoers, with cups of wine that painted my lips red, with smoke from menthol cigarettes; I was waiting for Gloria to finally approach me. Little by little, we were left alone in the old apartment she was using as an office. I helped her clean up and offered to give her a ride home.

Her exhaustion, barely concealed by her habitual good manners, made me forget my questions. It was clear that she didn't want to talk to me. Our trip passed in almost total silence. When we arrived at her house, she gave me a kiss on the cheek with an unusual warmth, there was something of fondness and gratitude in it. She got out of the car and walked towards her front door. Her slender back was the last thing I saw before I drove off.

I read in the newspaper soon afterwards that Gloria had been murdered in that same house. She had been hung from the ceiling. The house was then set on fire. They never found the killers; according to the police report, there were more than two people involved. Gloria's body was completely charred. The newspaper articles on the case suggested that the hand of criminal organizations or police officers could be seen behind this atrocity.

On more than one occasion I've driven past the remains of that house, as it remained condemned for some time. I wanted to intuit the dimensions of the tragedy of my friend's appalling death in that ruined façade.

Death by fire has been in the mind of Mexico's sicarios and police officers for some time now.

Now, more than two decades since her unspeakable murder, my mind turns to Gloria, her smile, her warmth. After all, in these years of horror—and this is painful to admit—we lack any other way to comfort ourselves.

All I can do is recall the truth and challenge announced by Walter Benjamin: it is only for the sake of those without hope that hope is given to us.

Notes

1. This account of the events in Iguala that night is based on press reports and the court record. The author is especially indebted to the information provided by Anabel Hernández and Steve Fisher, *La historia no oficial*, *Proceso*, December 13, 2014, pp 6–11; John Gibler, who I heard speak on October 16th, 2014 and whose written account appears in The Disappeared, *The California Sunday Magazine*, January 2015, http://stories.californiasunday.com/2015-01-04/mexico-the-disappeared-en; and Marcela Turati, Ayotzinapa: sus propios informes comprometen al Ejército, *Proceso*, March 22, 2015, pp. 18–22; Juan Pablo Becerra-Acosta, No fue el Ejército, pero tampoco lo impidió, *Milenio*, February 2, 2015, http://www.milenio.com/firmas/juan_pablo_becerra-acosta/Ejercito-impidio_18_457334266.html. Another account of these events can be found in: Cuauhtémoc Contreras, La última noche de Ayotzinapa. Los 43 asesinados y el botín político, revistareplicante.com, undated, http://revistareplicante.com/la-ultima-noche-de-ayotzinapa; and Esteban Illades, La noche más triste, *nexos*, January 1, 2015, http://www.nexos.com.mx/?p=23809.

2. Articles 7, 28, 29 and 30 of the Rome Statute of the International Criminal Court, Supreme Court of Justice of the Nation, Mexico, 2005, 116 pp. This statute entered into force in Mexico on January 1, 2006. Retrieved from https://www.scjn.gob.mx/libro/InstrumentosEstatuto/PAG0453.pdf

3. *Univisión Música*, November 21, 2014, http://musica.univision.com/article/2166697/2014-11-21/latin-grammy/noticias/calle13-residente-ayotzinapa. In a comparative study of 59 countries,

Mexico was ranked as the country with one of the highest levels of impunity in the world, with an impunity index of 75.7—second only to the Philippines, which has an impunity index of 80. The source of these figures is the 2015 Global Impunity Index (University of the Americas—Puebla and Citizens' Council for Public Security and Criminal Justice): Dennis A. García, Alertan por niveles de impunidad en México, *El Universal*, April 21, 2015, http://www.eluniversal.com.mx/nacion-mexico/2015/alertan-por-niveles-de-impunidad-en-mexico-1093976.html.

4. Octavio Paz, *The Collected Poems of Octavio Paz, 1957–1987*, translated by Eliot Weinberger, New Directions, New York 1987.

5. Part of this information comes from Gibler, *op.cit.*, as well as from http://es.wikipedia.org/Escuela_Normal_Rural_de_Ayotzinapa.

6. The figures on poverty are taken from Medición de la pobreza en México y en las entidades federativas 2012, July 29, 2013, Interior Secretariat, 2013, 120 pp., http://www.coneval.org.mx/Medicion/Paginas/Medici%C3%B3n/Pobreza%202012/Pobreza-2012.aspx; also: http://eleconomista.com.mx/sociedad/2013/12/29/guerrero-mezcla-pobreza-e-inseguridad.

7. Cf. http://es.wikipedia.org/wiki/Estado_de_Guerrero and the official website of the state government: http://guerrero.gob.mx.

8. Humberto Musacchio, *Diccionario Enciclopédico de México, Ilustrado*, Vol. II, Mexico, edited by Andrés León, 1990, 798 pp.

9. Sergio González Rodríguez, *El hombre sin cabeza*, Barcelona, Anagrama, 2009, pg. 15.

10. Sergio González Rodríguez, Escalera al Cielo. Contracultura y disolución, *Reforma, Revista Cultural El Ángel*, October 18, 1998. Here we can read about the country's unprecedented *borderization*: "The present institutional crisis has reached a historical-cultural statute that demonstrates, day after day, an alarming fact: in our country, everything is becoming a border, a twilight zone in which anything can happen. A border that, in spite of the best efforts of civil society and institutions to find a dignified and viable means of coexistence, spreads the scourge of crime, impunity, the loss of respect for life, the disappearance of persons as an industry of

extermination […]. Empires—like nation-states—become decadent when they become unable to guarantee the integrity of their sovereignty and their territory. In recent years—due to ancestral inequality, the disaster of the globalized economy, the fall of the authoritarian presidency, the slow institution of a new political system, the drug trafficking boom, police and judicial corruption and the migration of workers—Mexico's borders have suffered from a series of perverse effects that tie together a multi-faceted erosion of everything from the national contract to public security."

11. Laura Castellanos, *México armado. 1943–1981*, Mexico, Ediciones Era, 2007, 383 pp, and: http://es.wikipedia.org/wiki/Ejército_Revolucionario_del_Pueblo_Insurgente; this site also contains a map of other guerrilla movements in Mexico.

12. Speech made by Subcomandante Marcos: http://www.bibliotecas.tv/sep94/15sep94.html.

13. ¿Qué es la FECSM? January 12, 2011, Facebook.com, http://www.facebook.com/notes/fecsm/qué-es-la-fecsm/101230406619809; Declaración de Principios de la FECSM, August 1, 2010, http://basesmagisteriales.blogspot.com.es/2010/08/declaracion-de-principios-de-la-fecsm.html; Guillermo Sheridan, Más lecturas sobre Ayotzinapa, *El Universal*, December 30, 2014, http://www.eluniversalmas.com.mx/editoriales/2014/12/74075.php.

14. The ERPI's manifesto can be found at http://www.enlace-erpi.org/tesis.html

15. Che Guevara, Socialism and Man in Cuba, https://www.marxists.org/archive/guevara/1965/03/man-socialism.htm

16. Sergio Ocampo Arista, Matan policías a dos estudiantes al desalojar un bloqueo carretero, *La Jornada*, December 13, 2011: http://www.jornada.unam.mx/2011/12/13/politiac/002n1pol. The gas station employee was named Gonzalo Miguel Rivas Cámara.

17. Manuel García Tinoco, Padre pedirá cuentas a líderes normalistas, *Excélsior*, November 20, 2014: http://www.excelsior.com.mx/nacional/2014/11/20/993386. On the ties between dissident teachers and guerrillas: Raymundo Rivas Palacio, Guerrero: empezó la insurrección (IV y fin): http://www.ejecentral.com.mx/

guerrero-empezo-la-insurreccion-iv-y-fin. Rivas Palacio states: "A Center for Research and National Security (CISEN) document shows that the EPR and the EPRI, together with their front organizations, are mobilizing with the State Coordinator of Education Workers of Guerrero (CETEG), the community police and some of the radical clergy to promote the consolidation of the *Line of Hope*, a political project that encompasses the indigenous belt that crosses Chiapas, Oaxaca and Guerrero. The Coordinator's dissident teachers are the most active part of this insurrection." The government has identified the following radical leaders behind the Ayotzinapa movement: Ramos Reyes Guerrero (CETEG), Pedro Eligio Cabañas (the brother of Lucio Cabañas), Taurino Rojas Florencio, Andreu Castañeda, Minervino Morán, Omar Garibay Guerra, Ubaldo Segura Pantoja, Bertoldo Martínez Cruz, Abel Barrera, Vidulfo Rosales, Ernesto Gallardo, Gonzalo Torres, Crisóforo García, Manuel Olivares, among others (ibid).

18. Rithy Panh and Christophe Bataille, *The Elimination*, New York, Other Press, 2013, p. 118 and ss.; Michel Onfray, *El sueño de Eichmann*, Barcelona, Gedisa, 2009, 92 pp.

19. On the issue of kidnapping, María Teresa Camarillo and Martha Álvarez (coord.), *El secuestro en México durante la primera década del siglo XXI*, Mexico, UNAM, undated, 32 pp.: http://bd.iib.unam.mx/secuestro/introduccion.pdf; also, Humberto Padgett, *Jauría. El secuestro en México*, Mexico, Grijalbo, 2010, 473 pp.

20. The idea of anti-institutional synergy is explained in Víctor Hugo Michel and Javier Trujillo, Guerrero: 'narco,' guerrilla and gangs in 62 municipalities, *Milenio*, November 24, 2014: http://www.milenio.com/policia/En_Guerrero_hay_presencia_de_narco_guerrilla_446666y_bandas_en_62_municipios_0_415158485.html; the declarations of José Luis Hernández Rivera, the director of the Ayotzinapa Rural Teachers' College, are quoted in: Lourdes Chávez, Al plantel "no entran delincuentes," responde el director de la Normal de Ayotzinapa, *El Sur*, October 30, 2014: http://suracapulco.mx/archivos/222441.

21. Sergio Rincón, Informe: gobiernos, criminales y actores sociales cercan al periodismo en Guerrero, sinembargo.mx, April 27, 2015: http://www.sinembargo.mx/27-04-2015/1326561.

22. Roberto Ramírez Bravo, Guerrero, de donde salen más migrantes a EU y norte del país, *La Jornada*, October 13, 2007: http://www.lajornadaguerrero.com.mx/2007/10/31/index.pho?section=sociedad&article=005n1soc.

23. FAR-LP: Aparece en México nuevo grupo guerrillero, deinformado.net, December 3, 2013: http://desinformado.net/far-lp-aparece-en-mexico-nuevo-grupo-guerrillero/. The FAR-LP's communiqué can be found at: http://cedema.org/ver.php?id=6398.

24. Video: ERPI declara la guerra a "Guerreros Unidos," aristeguinoticias.com, October 9, 2014: http://aristeguinoticias.com/0910/mexico/video-erpi-declara-la-guerra-a-guerreros-unidos/.

25. Ciudadanos de Guerrero reprueban a gobierno: encuesta, lasillarota.com, February 12, 2015: http://lasillarota.com/reprueban-a-autoridades-por-caso-ayotzinapa-gce#.VVsPKKat07h; the Chamber of Deputies also conducted a study showing that 71% of those surveyed are somewhat or very sympathetic to the protests for the 43; the majority of those who are aware of the protests (85%) have not participated, and of them 40% would be willing to participate while 48% would never participate under any circumstances: National Public Opinion Survey: The Case of the Ayotzinapa Rural Teachers' School, Chamber of Deputies, LXII Legislature/Social Studies and Public Opinion Center, Mexico, December 2014, 32 pp.

26. Francisco Magaña, Acusa Rogelio Ortega a normalistas de haber cobrado de 30 a 80 millones de pesos en casetas, *El Sur*, January 28, 2015: http://suracapulco.mx/archivos/248344; Normalistas egresados roban vehículos oficiales y de empresas transnacionales, Agencia Informativa Guerrero, November 14, 2014: http://www.agenciainformativaguerrero.com/?p=26127.

27. The activist's name is Gustavo Rodríguez Romero. Gustavo Castillo and Emir Olivares, Anticastrista deportado del país, ideólogo de anarquistas, *La Jornada*, December 4, 2014: http://www.lajornada.unam.mx/ultimas/2014/12/04/anti-castrista-deportado-del-pais-ideologo-de-anarquistas-560.html. The country's most important anarchist groups include Okupa Che,

Cruz Negra, Anarquistas de México, Coordinadora Estudiantil Anarquista and Instinto Salvaje.

28. Georges Didi-Huberman, *La imagen superviviente. Historia del arte y tiempo de los fantasmas según Aby Warburg*, Madrid, Abada, 2009, p. 106.

29. Saúl Hernández, Combate a narco deja 403 soldados muertos, *El Universal*, February 19, 2014: http://www.eluniversal.com.mx/nacion-mexico/2014/impreso/soldados-ms-paga-ms-riesgo-44444.html.

30. Víctor Ballinas, La CNDH asegura que 250 personas fueron *eje-cutadas* durante la *guerra sucia*, *La Jornada*, November 4, 2001: http://www.jornada.unam.mx/2001/11/04/012n1pol.html.

31. Misael Habana de los Santos, López Betancourt: personas vivas fueron tirados desde aviones en la *guerra sucia*, *La Jornada*, November 30, 2003: http://wwww.jornada.unam.mx/2003/11/30/012n4pol.php?origen=index.html&fly=1.

32. CMDPDH, El caso Rosendo Radilla Pacheco, Mexico, Mexican Commission for the Defense and Promotion of Human Rights (CMDPDH), 2014: http://cmdpdh.org/casos-paradigmaticos-2-2/casos-defendidos/caso-rosendo-radilla-pacheco-2/.

33. According to the non-governmental organization México Evalúa, there were 101,000 homicides of all types in Mexico between 2006 and 2012, a figure that resembles the number of casualties during the wars in Iraq and the Balkans: Rolando Herrera, Estiman 101 mil asesinados en sexenio, Agencia Reforma, November 27, 2012: http://www.elmanana.com/estiman101mila sesinadosensexenio-1861268.html; Robert Sandels, Militarization and Political Crisis in Mexico, Global Research, September 4, 2013: http://www.globalresearch.ca/militarization-and-political-crisis-in-mexico/5347998.

34. Homero Campa, En este sexenio, 13 desaparecidos al día, *Proceso*, February 8, 2015, pp. 8–19: http://www.proceso.com.mx/?p=393506. Also: Federico Mastrogiovanni, *Ni vivos ni muertos*, Mexico, Grijalbo, 2014, 232 pp.

35. Nick Turse, *Kill Anything That Moves: The Real American War in Vietnam*, New York, Picador, 2013, 416 pp.

36. Alberto Morales, Segob precisa cifra de desaparecidos, ascienden a 16 mil, *El Universal*, June 16, 2014: http://www.eluniversal.com.mx/nacion-mexico/2014/segob-precisa-cifra-de-desaparecidos-ascienden-a-16-mil-1017375.html; also, Notimex, CNDH reporta 27 mil desaparecidos en México, cifra cerca a la de Segob, aristeguinoticias.com, June 5, 2013: http://aristeguinoticias.com/ 0506/mexico/cndh-reporta-27-mil-desaparecidos/.

37. The author is especially grateful to Marcela Turati for the information provided in: Marcela Turati, Iguala-Cocula-Taxco: el corredor de las desapariciones, *Proceso*, December 14, 2014, 16–18 pp: http://www.proceso.com.mx/?p=390561.

38. Extract from a poem by David Huerta titled Ayotzinapa: http://www.tierraadentro.conaculta.gob.mx/ayotzinapa-de-david-huerta/.

39. Giorgio Agamben, *Remnants of Auschwitz: The Witness and the Archive*, New York, Zone Books, 1999, 176 pp.

40. Ibid, pg. 12.

41. Verónica Macías, La violencia domina en 20 municipios; 5 son del Edomex, *El Economista*, February 6, 2014: http://eleconomista.com.mx/sociedad/2014/02/06/violencia-domina-20-municipios-5-son-edomex.

42. Notimex, Encabeza Guerrero cifras de violencia contra la mujer, *Crónica*, March 8, 2011: http://www.cronica.com.mx/notas/2011/564919.html.

43. These figures and the analysis on the homicide rate in Guerrero over time is taken from the excellent report: SJP, Guerrero, atrapados en el círculo de la violencia, Mexico, Seguridad, Justicia y Paz/Consejo Ciudadano para la Seguridad Pública y Justicia Penal A.C., 2014, pg. 10 and ff.: http://editor.pbsiar.com/upload/PDF/guerrero.pdf

44. Jesús Ramírez Cuevas, Policías comunitarios, grupos de autodefensa y paramilitares, *La Jornada del Campo*, May 18, 2013: http://www.jornada.unam.mx/2013/05/18/cam-grupos.html.

45. Mauricio Torres, Grupos de autodefensa operan en 46 de 81 municipios de Guerrero: CNDH, CNN México, December 17, 2013: http://mexico.cnn.com/nacional/2013/12/17/la-cndh-advierte-que-los-grupos-de-autodefensa-agravan-la-inseguridad.

46. A collection of popular verses from the Costa Chica of Guerrero and Oaxaca can be found at: http://costachica nuestra.blogspot.mx/2009/07/versos-costenos.html.

47. Cf. the report of the SJP, *op. cit.*, p. 121. Between 2005 and 2013, the homicide rate rose by 435%, with 4.07 kidnappings per 100,000 residents in 2013, 179% above the national average. In 2013, Iguala was in eighth place in the Municipal Violence Index with 52.25 points, more than double the national average (23.17 points).

48. Pineda, operadora de 'Guerreros Unidos' en gobierno municipal. Red Política, October 22, 2014: http://www.redpolitica.mx/nacion/pineda-operadora-de-guerreros-unidos-en-gobierno-municipal; Abarca's wealth and political connections grew to such an extent in such a short time that in 2008 he opened a four-hectare shopping mall, known as Galería Tamarindos, home to major corporations such as McDonald's, Cinepolis, Mega Comercial Mexicana, Coppel, etc. Part of the land on which the mall was constructed had been donated by the Defense Secretariat: Ángel Cabrera, Los Abarca tuvieron apoyo politico para construir Galería Tamarindos, *24 Horas*, November 27, 2014: http://www.24-horas.mx/los-abarca-tuvieron-apoyo-politico-para-construir-galerias-tamarindos/.

49. Revela Reforma: AMLO apoyó a Abarca a pesar de denuncias contra el exalcalde de Iguala, sdpnoticias.com, October 26, 2014: http://www.sdpnoticias.com/nacional/2014/10/26/revela-reforma-amlo-apoyo-a-abarca-a-pesar-de-denuncias-contra-el-exalcalde-de-iguala.

50. Sergio González Rodríguez, *El hombre sin cabeza*, *op. cit.*, p. 23.

51. The non-governmental organization Causa en Común A.C. has prepared an excellent report titled Radiografía de las organizaciones criminales que operan en Guerrero; this is the source of the facts and analysis cited herein. It can be found at: Ciudadanos en Red, Mexico, November 24, 2014: http://ciudadanosenred.com.mx/infopractica/radiografia-de-las-organizaciones-criminales-que-operan-en-guerrero/. According to this report, at the end of 2014 Los Rojos controlled 37 municipalities; La Familia Michoacana, 31; Guerreros Unidos, 30; Knights Templar, 18; La Barredora, 10; the Jalisco New Generation Cartel, 10; the Independent Cartel of Acapulco, 10; Los Ardillos, 8; Los Granados, 6; and, lastly, The Sinaloa/Pacific Cartel, 2 (this cartel has an alliance with La Barredora, which it uses to exert its influence on the Costa Chica).

52. Reuters, Controlan *Caballeros templarios* la exportación de mineral de hierro, *La Jornada*, January 3, 2014: http://www.jornada.unam.mx/2014/01/03/politica/005n1pol; Raymundo Riva Palacio, Ahumada, su narcomina y los chinos, ejecentral.com.mx, January 9, 2015: http://wwww.ejecentral.com.mx/ahumada-su-narcomina-y-los-chinos/.

53. On the factors that can lead to war in the contemporary world: Joan Esteban, Laura Mayoral and Debraj Ray, Ethnicity and Conflict: Theory and Facts, *Science*, USA, May 18, 2012, vol. 336, pp. 858–865.

54. Arturo Ángel, 31 millones de delitos quedaron en impunidad durante 2013, INEGI, 24-horas.mx, September 30, 2014: http://www.24-horas.mx/31-millones-de-delitos-quedaron-en-impunidad-durante-2013-inegi/.

55. One example of how the government manipulates its data can be seen in: Humberto Padgett, Así se maquillan las cifras de inseguridad en el EDOMEX, sinembargo.com, March 31, 2015: http://www.sinembargo.mx/31-03-2015/1297853.

56. An extract from Henry Kissinger's speech can be found at http://www.elfinanciero.com.mx/opinion/henry-kissinger-su-vision-sobre-mexico-hoy.html; Henry Kissinger, *World Order: Reflections on the Character of Nations and the Course of History*, New York, Penguin Press, 2014, 432 pp.

57. Cf., Jenaro Villamil, Mala imagen de EPN, pese al dispendio en promoción, *Proceso*, August 31, 2014: http://www.proceso.com.mx/?p=380913.

58. The effects of NAFTA and the figures cited herein are analyzed in an excellent article by Christy Thornton and Adam Goodman, How the Mexican Drug Trade Thrives on Free Trade, *The Nation*, July 15, 2014: http://www.thenation.com/article/180587/how-mexican-drug-trade-thrives-free-trade; the author would also like to thank Adam Goodman for his generosity on this matter.

59. The magazine *Esquire Latin America* published this report; see also: Tlatlaya: Cronología básica, del 30 de junio al 21 de octubre, aristeguinoticias.com, October 22, 2014: http://aristeguinoticias.com/2210/mexico/cronologia-del-caso-tlatlaya-desde-el-30-de-junio-al-21-de-octubre/.

60. Encubre Edomex masacre militar, *Proceso*, January 1, 2015. On the Code Red combat protocol: Juan Veledíaz, Tlatlaya: ¿orden roja?, estadomayor.mx, October 1, 2014: http://estadomayor.mx/47379.

61. Emir Olivares Alonso, La tortura persiste en México y es tolerada por autoridades, *La Jornada*, September 4, 2014: http://www.jornada.unam.mx/2014/09/04/politica/008n1pol; Citlal Giles Sánchez, México, el segundo país donde más se violan derechos humanos, reporta la ONU, *La Jornada*, February 6, 2011: http://www.lajornadadeguerrero.com.mx/2011/02/06/index.php?section=sociedad&article=005n1so; EFE, Tortura en México es generalizada refrenda relator de ONU; hubo presión para minimizar, April 3, 2015: http://www.24-horas.mx/tortura-en-mexico-es-generalizada-refrenda-relator-de-onu-revela-presiones-para-minimizarla/; Notimex and Eugenia Jiménez, México pide a ONU pruebas de "tortura generalizada," *Milenio*, April 2, 2015: http://www.milenio.com/politica/ONU_tortura_Mexico-informe_tortura_Mexico_0_492550755.html.

62. INEGI, Estadísticas a propósito del Día de muertos (2 de noviembre), Aguascalientes, México, October 30, 2014, National Institute of Statistics and Geography: http://noticieros.televisa.com/mexico/140/estadisticas-proposito-dia-muertos.

63. Norberto Bobbio, *Democracia y secreto*, Mexico, FCE, 2013, p. 49.

64. Cf., Marcela Turati, San Fernando-Ayotzinapa: las similitudes, *Proceso*, December 21, 2014: http://www.proceso.com.mx/?p=391273; also: http://es.wikipedia.org/wiki/2010_San_Fernando_massacre. On the barbarism in Apatzingán: Laura Castellanos, Las ejecuciones de Apatzingán: policías federales, los autores, *Proceso*, April 19, 2015, 12–19 pp.: http://www.proceso.com.mx/?p=401646.

65. Sergio González Rodríguez, *El robo del siglo*, Mexico, Grijablo, 2015, pp. 128–132.

66. Natalia Gómez Quintero, Ayotzinapa no representa fracaso en cooperación: EU, *El Universal*, February 3, 2015: http://www.eluniversal.com.mx/nacion-mexico/2015/ayotzinapa-no-representa-un-fracaso-en-cooperacion-eu-1074086.html.

67. Through the CIA, the United States government carries out "activities" (covert operations) that stimulate *focos* of institutional destabilization in Mexican territory by means of criminal organizations, which allows for real combat scenarios against anti-institutional groups and training for the armed forces and maintains their control of the territory by means of geopolitical pressure. See Sergio González Rodríguez, *Campo de Guerra*, Barcelona, Anagrama, 2014, p. 24 and following.

68. On Guerrero's gold deposits, Notimex, En Guerrero, la mina más grande de América Latina, *Crónica*, February 11, 2013: http://www.cronica.com.mx/notas/2005/212974.html.

69. Eduardo Esquivel, La minería en México, un negocio para pocos, sdpnoticias.com, May 8, 2013: http://www.sdpnoticias.com/columnas/2013/05/08/la-mineria-en-mexico-un-negocio-para-pocos.

70. José Guaderrama, Heroína mexicana, la "preferida" en EU, *El Universal*, October 3, 2014: http://www.eluniversal.com.mx/nacion-mexico/2014/impreso/heroina-mexicana-la-8216preferida-8217-en-eu-219066.html.

71. Alberto Sicilia Falcón's history with the CIA can be seen in Peter Dale Scott and Jonathan Marshall, *Cocaine Politics: Drugs, Armies, and the CIA in Central America*, Berkeley, University of California Press, 1998, p. 33 and following; see also: Froylán

Enciso, Alberto Sicilia Falcón, el narcostar bisexual, nuestraa-parenterendicion.com, February 10, 2012: http://nuestraa-parenterendicion.com/index.php/blogs-nar/weary-bystanders/item/946-alberto-sicilia-falc%C3%B3n-el-narcostar-bisexual.

72. On Mexico's Operation Condor: Diego Osorno, *El cártel de Sinaloa*, México, Grijalbo, 2009, eBook edition, p. 96 and following.

73. On the CIA's global destabilization activities: *CIA Activities in the Americas*, Memphis, Books LLC, 2010, 95 pp.; Tim Weiner, *Legacy of Ashes: The History of the CIA*, New York, Anchor, 2008, 848 pp.; Mark Mazzetti, *The Way of the Knife: The CIA, a Secret Army, and a War at the Ends of the Earth*, New York, Penguin Press, 2013, 381 pp. See also the following chronology: http://marting.stormpages.com/laciayel.htm; and, for a recent episode from Latin America: http://noticierostelevisa.esmas.com/internacional/520896/correa-retoma-denuncia-operacion-cia-desestabilizar-gobierno/. According to the DEA agents operating in Mexico at the time, the CIA carried out the assassinations of Manuel Buendía and Enrique "Kiki" Camarena: J. Jesús Esquivel, La historia secreta detrás del asesinato de Camarena, *Proceso*, October 19, 2013: http://www.proceso.com. mx/?p=355922. On covert US operations in Mexico and around the world: John Jacob Nutter, *The CIA's Black Ops: Covert Action, Foreign Policy, and Democracy*, Amherst, Prometheus Books, 1999, 361 pp.; L. Fletcher Prouty, *The Secret Team: The CIA and Its Allies in Control of the United States and the World*, New York, Skyhorse Publishing, 2011, 480 pp. On Operation Gladio: Daniele Ganser, Cuando el juez Felice Casson reveló la existencia de Gledio…: http://www.voltairenet.org/article 163083.html; Anna Grau, La CIA se dedica al asesinato selectivo, *ABC*, March 8, 2010: http://www.abc.es/20100308/internacional-internacional/dedica-asesinato-selectivo-20100308.html.

74. Jorge Carrasco Araizaga, El gobierno de Calderón acordó con el de Obama el tráfico ilegal de armas, *Proceso*, March 22, 2013, pp. 24–30: http://www.proceso.com.mx/?p=399068; http://es.wikipedia.org/ wiki/Escándalos_de_ventas_de_armas_en_Estados_Unidos_a_cárteles_mexicanos; Peña propone que agentes extranjeros puedan portar armas en territorio mexicano, animal politico.com, February 24, 2015: http://www.animalpolitico.com/

2015/02/pena-propone-que-agentes-extranjeros-puedan-portar-armas-en-territorio-mexicano.

75. Carlos Fazio, La intervención y la entrega, *La Jornada*, March 2, 2015: http://www.jornada.unam.mx/archivo_opinion/autor/front/48/44424; Raymundo Riva Palacio, Tres Marías, espías en conflicto, *El Financiero*, August 22, 2014: http://www.elfinanciero.com.mx/opinion/tres-marias-espias-en-conflicto.html; J. Jesús Esquivel, Armamentismo en tiempos de Peña Nieto, *Proceso*, March 28, 2015, pp. 6–9: http://www.proceso.com.mx/399699/armamentismo-en-tiempos-de-pena-nieto; Peña Nieto ha comprado armas "sin precedentes" a EU: más de 3 mil mdd, animalpolitico.com, June 16, 2015: http://www.animalpolitico.com/2015/06/pena-nieto-ha-comprado-armas-sin-precedentes-a-eu-mas-de-3-mil-mdd/.

76. Jorge Fernández Menéndez, *Narcotráfico y poder*, Mexico, Rayuela, pp. 19 and following.

77. Mark Mazzetti, *The Way of the Knife: The CIA, a Secret Army, and a War at the Ends of the Earth*, New York, Penguin Press, 2013, 381 pp.

78. Robert Chesney, Military-Intelligence Convergence and the Law of the Title 10/Title 50 Debate, *Journal of Security Law and Policy*, 2012, pp. 539–629: http://jnslp.com/wp-content/uploads/2012/01/Military-Intelligence-Convergence-and-the-Law-of-the-Title-10Title-50-Debate.pdf

79. Jefferson Morley, *Our Man in Mexico: Winston Scott and the Hidden History of the CIA*, Lawrence, Kansas University Press, 2014, 503 pp., p. 90 and following. The code names of these agents were: LITENSOR, LITEMPO-2, LITEMPO-8 and LITEMPO-4; also: Jefferson Morley, LITEMPO: los ojos de la CIA en Tlatelolco: http://nsarchive.gwu.edu/NSAEBB/NSAEBB204/index2.htm: "The letters LI was the agency's code for operations based in Mexico; TEMPO was the term given by Scott for a program that, in the words of a secret history of the agency, was 'a productive and effective relationship between the CIA and select top officials in Mexico.' Initiated in 1960, LITEMPO functioned as 'an unofficial channel for the exchange of selected sensitive political information which each government wanted the other to receive but not through public

protocol exchanges.' In the CIA archives, Scott's agents were identified with specific numbers." See also: Philip Agee, *Inside the
Company: CIA Diary*, New York, Farrar, Straus and Giroux, 1975,
639 pp.: https://leaksource.files.wordpress.com/ 2014/08/inside-
the-company-cia-diary-philip-agee.pdf.

80. Scott and Marshall, *op. cit.*

81. Enciso, *op. cit.*

82. Rafael Rodríguez Castañeda, *El policía. Perseguía, torturaba,
mataba*, Mexico, Grijalbo, 2013, 146 pp.

83. Speech by CIA Director John O. Brennan, sponsored by the
Council on Foreign Relations. US Intelligence in a Transforming
World. CIA's Global Mission: Countering Shared Threats, March
13, 2015: http://www.cfr.org/intelligence/us-intelligence-trans-
forming-world/p36271.

84. SJP, Rogelio Ortega Martínez, el flamante gobernador interino
de Guerrero, es un secuestrador ligado a las FARC, seguridadjustici-
aypaz.org.mx, October 24, 2014: http://www.seguridadjusticiay-
paz.org.mx/sala-de-prensa/1115-rogelio-ortega-martinez-el-fla-
mante-gobernador-interino-de-guerrero-es-un-secuestrador-liga-
do-a-las-farc. The interim governor of Guerrero appointed after
the resignation of Ángel Aguirre Rivero, Rogelio Ortega Martínez,
has been accused of being part of the connection between
Guerrero's guerrilla organizations and the FARC-EP and of carrying
out kidnappings in support of the revolutionary cause. He has
denied this accusation, which the Mexican government has not
investigated. On the connections between Colombian guerrillas
and Al-Qaeda: Las FARC usan redes de Al Qaeda para introducir
cocaína en Europa, *Semana*, October 12, 2014: http://www.sem-
ana.com/nacion/articulo/farc-usan-redes-de-al-qaeda-para-intro-
ducir-cocaina-en-europa/411647-3.

85. JCS, United States Department of the Army, et al, *Counterinsurgency*, November 22, 2013, p. ix and following: http://www.-
dtic.mil/doctrine/new_pubs/jp3_24.pdf.

86. Ibid.

87. Ibid.

88. Colombia recuerda a 43 víctimas de matanza atribuida a paramilitares en 1988, información.com, November 11, 2013:
http://noticias.lainformacion.com/disturbios-conflictos-y-guer-
ra/matanza/colombia-recuerda-a-43-victimas-de-matanza-atribui-
da-a-paramilitares-en-1988_C1oaQ6dGiAy5FFOb5qiX64/;
http://es.wikipedia.org/wiki/Masacre_de_El_Salado; The Red
Phoenix, Cold War Killer File: The Death Squads of El Salvador—
Part 1, August 12, 2012: http://theredphoenixapl.org/
2012/08/12/cold-war-killer-file-the-death-squads-of-el-salvador-
part-1/.

89. United States Department of the Army, Army Tactical
Standard Operating Procedures, November 2011, pp. 1–4:
http://armypubs.army.mil/doctrine/DR_pubs/dr_a/pdf/atp3_90x
90.pdf

90. On the counterinsurgency narrative: JCS, United States
Department of the Army, et al, *Counterinsurgency*, *op. cit.*

91. Ciro Gómez Leyva, Entrevista a José Luis Abarca. "Se lava las
manos" por masacre de normalistas, polakastv, September 29,
2014: https://www.youtube.com/watch?v=FP22lztQ33E. Also:
telephone conversation between the interior secretary of Guerrero
and José Luis Abarca hours after the massacre in Iguala: https://
www.youtube.com/watch?v=XTBF5MHpA8I. Also: Hernández and
Fisher, La historia no official, *op. cit.* The author would like to
thank Juan Veledíaz for his generous help in obtaining the information in question from the National Defense Secretariat.
Douglas Valentine, *The Phoenix Program: America's Use of Terror in
Vietnam*, New York, Open Road Media, 2014, 486 pp.; also:
http://www.unwelcomeguests.net/693_-_Social_Destabilization_
Tactics_Post_WW2_(From_Operation_Phoenix_to_the_War_On
_ Terror).

92. Víctor Hugo Michel, EU impartió 7.678 cursos a militares
mexicanos de élite, milenio.com, April 3, 2015: http://www.mile-
nio.com/policia/EU-impartio-cursos-militares-mexicanos_
0_493150716.html. Also: http://en.wikipedia.org/wiki/Counter-
terrorism. On Colonel Juan Antonio Aranda: Luis Hernández

Navarro, La matanza de Iguala y el ejército, *La Jornada*, November 18, 2014: http://www.jornada.unam.mx/2014/11/18/opinion/017a2pol. The 27th Battalion has a history of atrocities that goes back to the dirty war in Guerrero four decades ago, which made use of counterinsurgency tactics employed in Vietnam; see Juan Veledíaz, De la "aldea vietnamita" a las "narco-fosas," estado-mayor.org, November 4, 2014: http://estadomayor.mx/48503. He writes: "With the arrival of Colonel Juan Antonio Aranda Flores in the fall of 2011, citizens of Iguala and surrounding towns began to report that their relatives were being deprived of their freedom. Rumors multiplied exponentially of death squads composed of highly trained individuals wearing black clothes and ski masks and armed with high caliber weapons. Testimonies collected by the local press indicate that these groups engaged in shootouts and operations to eliminate people from rival criminal organizations. They were distinguished by their attire, their appearance and their use of high caliber weapons [...]. When Colonel José Rodríguez Pérez relieved Aranda Flores of command of the battalion in 2013, suspicions of possible ties between soldiers and the criminal organization Guerreros Unidos only increased"; see also: Juan Veledíaz, La película prohibida del batallón 27, estadomayor.org, November 21, 2014: http://estadomayor.mx/49180. The National Defense Secretariat has declined to release the name of the undercover soldier who was among the 43, claiming that it is classified information, although unofficial accounts indicate that there were two undercover soldiers, one of them being Julio César López Patolzin: Ezequiel Flores Contreras, El enigma del soldado-normalista desaparecido, *Proceso*, June 21, 2015, pp. 32–33. Spokespeople for the disappeared students have denied this information, blaming the army for the disappearance of the 43 and demanding clarification on the true role of Captain José Martínez Crespo of the 27th Infantry Battalion. The father of José Martínez Crespo has admitted that his son was a soldier before he enrolled in the Ayotzinapa Rural Teachers' College: Ezequiel Flores Contreras, Padre de uno de los 43 admite que su hijo fue military, pero "desertó," *Proceso*, June 22, 2015: http://proceso.com.mx/?p=408442. On the elite police in Iguala: Los Bélicos, pieza clave del ataque a normalistas, *Proceso*, June 21, 2015, pp. 30-32: http://www.proceso.com.mx/?p=408162.

93. The name of this source, as well as their exact profession, have been omitted at their request. On the activities of US soldiers and undercover agents in Mexico, Devlin Barrett, US Marshals Service Personnel Dressed as Mexican Marines Pursue Cartel Bosses: http://www.wsj.com/articles/u-s-marshals-service-personnel-dressed-as-mexican-marines-pursue-drug-cartel-bosses-1416595305; Agentes de EU operan en México disfrazados de militares nacionales: WJS, *La Jornada*, November 21, 2014: http://www.jornada.unam.mx/ultimas/2014/11/21/agentes-estadunidenses-disfrazados-de-militares-mexicanos-participan-en-operativos-antinarcoticos-wsj-9105.html; also: Ginger Thompson, US Widens Role in Battle Against Mexican Drug Cartels: http://www.nytimes.com/2011/08/07/world/07drugs.html?page-wanted=all&_r=0; Operan en México agentes de la CIA y la DEA, señala el NYT, *La Jornada*, August 8, 2011: http://www.jornada.unam.mx/2011/08/08/politica/002n1pol; Ciro Pérez Silva, Agentes de la FBI ayudaron en la indignatoria del caso Ayotzinapa, *La Jornada*, December 20, 2014: http://www.jornada.unam.mx/2014/12/20/politica/005n1pol.

94. Gustavo Castillo García, No ha habido desistimiento en el caso de federales que balearon a agentes de la CIA, *La Jornada*, August 22, 2014: http://www.jornada.unam.mx/2014/08/22/politi-ca/006n1pol.

95. Reuters, Popularidad de Peña, en su peor nivel como presidente, *El Economista*, December 1, 2014: http://eleconomista.com.mx/sociedad/2014/12/01/popularidad-pena-nieto-cae-nivel-mas-bajo.

96. Éstos son los diez puntos que anunció Peña Nieto en respuesta al caso Ayotzinapa, November 28, 2014, animalpolitico.com: http://www.animalpolitico.com/2014/11/pena-nieto-acuerdo-seguridad-comision-anuncio-mensaje-palacio-nacional/. His ten-point plan is as follows:

1. A proposed law aiming to prevent the infiltration of municipal authorities by criminal organizations (as if there weren't already laws in Mexico that punished this, such as the Federal Law Against Organized Crime).

2. A proposed constitutional reform that would redefine criminal jurisdictions (even though there are already clear definitions of said jurisdictions, such as in the 2013–2018 National Development Plan, as well as the fact that the problem is inefficiency and incompetence, not jurisdiction).

3. Elimination of municipal police forces, which will be replaced by a system of unified police commands at the state level (he must believe that it's enough to dissolve municipal police forces to end corruption and ineptitude among public servants, because this proposal includes nothing on how this would improve police work aside from merely centralizing command).

4. A national emergency number. It will be the Mexican 911 (the arguments used to support this proposal emphasize that it will help the authorities to immediately respond to emergencies; response times are currently poor despite the variety of emergency numbers available).

5. A national identification number for citizens (nobody can explain how or why this would correct the problems of the systems currently being used to identify citizens for tax, penal, census, consular, professional or electoral purposes).

6. An immediate police operation in the Tierra Caliente region of Guerrero and Michoacán (again, this is simply an operation to "pacify" the region, like so many others that came before it in years past and that have failed to bring peace and security, instead only managing to polarize Mexico's urban and rural communities).

7. Additional reforms with the goal of making the criminal justice system more accessible to victims (victims' rights in Mexico are a bureaucratic and legislative pipe dream; additional reforms will only add functional obstacles, apart from the fact that, despite the changeover from an inquisitorial system to the accusatorial-adversarial system imposed by the US government, the judicial system continues to reproduce vices that prevent an end to impunity).

8. General laws on torture and forced disappearance; improving protocols for cases of torture, forced disappearance and extrajudicial executions; creation of a database of missing persons and another for genetic information (again, new laws and

protocols are announced when there are already adequate laws and protocols and the problem is in their implementation).

9. A fight against corruption (once again we see the creation of new bureaucratic-political organisms that tend to reproduce the problem instead of providing a solution).

10. An information portal on government contractors and suppliers (an information portal like this already exists and this proposal includes no measures to prevent favoritism in contracts and licitations, nor on the burden of illicit commissions for contractors, suppliers and even government employees).

Days later, a security plan was announced: Sergio Ocampo Arista, Fuerzas federales asumen tareas de seguridad en Tierra Caliente, *La Jornada*, December 4, 2014: http://www.jornada.unam.mx/2014/12/04/politica/003n1pol.

97. Raimundo Riva Palacio, Ayotzinapa, penetrada por Los Rojos, *El Financiero*, May 1, 2015: http://www.elfinanciero.com.mx/opinion/ayotzinapa-penetrada-por-los-rojos.html.

98. Las pruebas dan certeza legal sobre la muerte de los normalistas: PGR, CNN, January 27, 2015: http://mexico.cnn.com/nacional/2015/01/27/el-testimonio-de-el-cepillo-refuerza-idea-de-muerte-de-normalistas-pgr.

99. Forzar la evidencia para que encaje con el testimonio, eso no es ciencia: peritos argentinos, aristeguinoticias.com, February 9, 2015: http://aristeguinoticias.com/0902/mexico/pgr-usa-ciencia-para-cuadrar-testimonios-peritos-argentinos/.

100. Rubicela Morelos, Descubren fraude en crematorio de Acapulco tras hallar 60 cuerpos, *La Jornada*, February 7, 2015: http://www.jornada.unam.mx/2015/02/07/politica/003n1pol.

101. Anabel Hernández, Ayotzinapa: la reconstrucción de los hechos confirma la presencia de la PF, *Proceso*, March 29, 2015, pp. 14–16: http://proceso.com.mx/?p=399676; Abel Barajas, Ordenan reponer proceso a Pineda Villa, reforma.com, April 27, 2015: http://www.reforma.com/aplicaciones/articulo/default.aspx?id=525761.

102. Procuraduría General de Justicia de Guerrero, September 27, 2014, Case File 172/2014-I, cited in: Hernández and Fisher, *op. cit.*

103. The request of the families of the 43 was directed to Santiago Mazari Hernández, *El Carrete*, who hung the banners in question around Morelos in February 2015: Jesús Guerrero, Piden ayuda a narco padres de normalistas, *Reforma*, April 1, 2015.

104. La Asamblea por Ayotzinapa acuerda boicotear elecciones; los padres llegan a Canadá, *El Sur*, April 12, 2015: http://www.sinembargo.mx/12-04-2015/1310250.

105. Extract from *La Formula Secreta* (1964) by Juan Rulfo. The text cited is taken from: Damián Ortega (ed.), *La formula secreta. Rubén Gámez*, Mexico, Alias, 2014, p. 29. The complete, definitive version of this text was established by the Juan Rulfo Foundation and Dylan Brennan.

106. The list of the 43 is taken from: http://es.wikipedia.org/wiki/Desaparición_forzada_en_Iguala_de_2014.

107. Miguel Ontiveros Alonso, La tragedia de Ayotzinapa a la luz de la dogmática penal, *El Mundo del Abogado*, vol. 16 no. 191, March 2, 2015, pp.42–47: http://elmundodelabogado.com/la-tragedia-de-ayotzinapa-a-la-luz-de-la-dogmatica-penal/. The author bases his position on publicly available information, as he did not have access to police records.

108. Murillo Karam's speech was transcribed by the newspaper *La Jornada* and published on its website on November 7, 2014: http://www.jornada.unam.mx/ultimas/2014/11/07/intervencion-del-procurador-de-la-republica-jesus-murillo-karam-durante-la-conferencia-de-prensa-para-exponer-el-caso-de-los-estudiantes-de-ayotzinapa-4374.html.

109. Ya me cansé: Murillo Karam explica esa frase tres días después, animalpolitico.com, November 11, 2014: http://www.animalpolitico.com/2014/11/ya-canse-murillo-karam-explica-esa-frase-tres-dias-despues/

110. Anabel Hernández and Steve Fisher, La pira que no se vio ni desde el aire, *Proceso*, December 21, 2014, pp. 12 and 13:

http://www.proceso.com/?p=391220. According to Jorge Montemayor, a researcher at the National Autonomous University of Mexico's Physics Institute, if the 43 students had been cremated in the Cocula garbage dump, there not only would have been remains of this funeral pyre, which would have either required 33 tons of firewood or 995 tires, which would have left behind 2.5 tons of steel wire, which nobody saw and the authorities failed to register in their inspections of the site. On the hypothesis that the victims were cremated and the refusal of the army to admit the existence of crematoria on their bases: Sanjuana Martínez, Sí hay crematorios en las instalaciones del Ejército, afirma el general Gallardo, *La Jornada*, January 11, 2015: http://www.jornada.unam.mx/2015/01/11/politica/007n1pol; Juan Pablo Becerra-Acosta, "Sí se pudo cremar" a los 43, *Milenio*, March 2, 2015: http://www.milenio.com/policia/Si_se_pudo_cremar_a_los_43-estudiantes_de_Ayotzinapa_pudieron_haber_sido_incinera-dos_0_473952631.html.

111. The officer in question is Alejandro Saavedra Hernández; Juan Veledíaz, Premian a generales de territorios en jaque, estado-mayor.mx, November 20, 2014: http://estadomayor.mx/49108.

112. Anabel Hernández, La reconstrucción de los hechos confirma la presencia de la PF, *op. cit.*

113. On the irregularities cited, the reports of the Interdisciplinary Group of Independent Experts (a creation of the Inter-American Commission on Human Rights) can be consulted at: http://centroprodh.org.mx/GIEI/?p=148; Expertos de CIDH denuncian "fragmentación" del caso Ayotzinapa, aristeguinoticias.com, May 11, 2015: http://aristeguinoticias.com/1105/mexico/expertos-de-cidh-denuncian-fragmentacion-del-caso-ayotzinapa/?code=reforma; "No vamos a permitir" que expertos de CIDH entrevisten al Ejército en Iguala: Osorio, aristeguinoticias.com, May 20, 2015: http://aristeguinoticias.com/2005/mexico/no-vamos-a-permitir-que-expertos-de-cidh-entrevisten-al-ejercito-en-iguala-osorio/?code=reforma.

Nota Bene: Some of the updated information in this edition comes from public domain sources, while others were released by *Proceso* magazine and the following sources:

Colectivo 43 Artes, *43. Una vida detrás de cada nombre* (Mexico, Xalapa, Universidad Veracruzana, 2015, 198 pp.); Francisco Cruz, et al, *La guerra que nos ocultan* (Mexico, Editorial Planeta, 2016, 376 pp.); John Gibler, *Una historia oral de la infamia* (Mexico, Editorial Grijalbo/Sur+, 2016, 232 pp.); Anabel Hernández, *La verdadera noche de Iguala*, Mexico, Editorial Grijalbo, 2016, 376 pp.). http://www.globalsecurity.org/military/agency/dod/soc-north.htm .

.

semiotext(e) intervention series